"Read this book!"

Cindy Sheehan
Founding member of Gold Star Families for Peace

"Many years ago in Korea, I believed I was serving a righteous cause. When reality jarred my assumptions, I first reacted angrily. My honor was offended. Then I met other ex-military who helped me understand that while my motives were good, the policies I was asked to support were not. We banded together to use our experience to help head off future wars through education. One of our most effective tools is *Addicted to War*."

Wilson (Woody) Powell*
Former Executive Director of Veterans for Peace

"The U.S., with 4.5% of the world's population, arrogantly plunders resources and cultures to support its American way of life. *Addicted to War* illustrates why the U.S. is *necessarily* dependent upon war to feed its shameful consumption patterns."

S. Brian Willson*
Vietnam veteran, anti-war activist

"I've come to the conclusion that if we don't change from a value system based on love of money and power to one based on love of compassion and generosity we will be extinct this century. We need a brief earthquake to wake up humanity. *Addicted to War* is such an earthquake."

Patch Adams, M.D.
Founder of Gesundheit Institute,
Vietnam War-era conscientious objector

"This is the most important comic book ever written. To be a true patriot (in the American revolutionary sense) is to understand the cruelty of U.S. foreign policy. Read this book and pass it on to as many people as you can."

Woody Harrelson
Actor

"War may be the 'health of the state,' as Randolph Bourne warned when a pacifist population was being driven to World War I by hysterical propaganda, but it is the curse of the people—the attackers and the victims. With spare and acid clarity, these snapshots of the real world brilliantly tell us why and how we must rid ourselves of this curse, quickly, or else descend to barbarism and destruction."

Noam Chomsky
Author and Professor Emeritus, MIT

*Served in the U.S. military

Why the U.S. Can't Kick Militarism

an illustrated exposé
by Joel Andreas

ISBN: 1-904859-01-1   ISBN13: 9781904859017

Requests to reprint all or part of *Addicted to War* should be addressed to:

Frank Dorrel   AK Press
P.O. Box 3261   674-A 23rd Street
Culver City, CA 90231-3261   Oakland, CA 94612-1163
(310) 838-8131   USA
fdorrel@addictedtowar.com   akpress@akpress.org
www.addictedtowar.com   www.akpress.org

To order more copies:

For information about ordering more copies of *Addicted to War*, contact either Frank Dorrel or AK Press. **Please ask about bulk rates!** *Addicted to War* is also available through your local bookstore and online book dealers. To receive an AK Press catalog, please write or visit the AK Press website.

To order *Addicted to War* in other languages:

A Spanish edition of *Addicted to War* has been published in the United States by Frank Dorrel and AK Press (please write to the addresses above). The book has also been translated into Japanese, Korean, Thai, Danish, and German, and soon will be available in other languages. To find out how to obtain copies of these translated editions, please visit: www.addictedtowar.com.

JOEL ANDREAS began following his parents to demonstrations against the Vietnam War while in elementary school in Detroit. He has been a political activist ever since, working to promote racial equality and workers' rights inside the United States and to stop U.S. military intervention abroad. After working as an automobile assembler, a printer, and a civil engineering drafter, he completed a doctoral degree in sociology at the University of California in Los Angeles, studying the aftermath of the 1949 Chinese Revolution. He now teaches at Johns Hopkins University in Baltimore. *Addicted to War* is Joel's third illustrated exposé. He wrote and drew *The Incredible Rocky,* an unauthorized biography of the Rockefeller family (which sold nearly 100,000 copies) while a student at Berkeley High School in California. He also wrote another comic book, *Made with Pure Rocky Mountain Scab Labor*, to support a strike by Coors brewery workers.

Table of Contents

Sources are listed starting on page 73 and are referenced throughout the book with circled numbers. All quotes in "quotation marks" are actual quotes.

Author's Preface to the 2004 Edition

I wrote the first edition of *Addicted to War* after the U.S. war against Iraq in 1991. The major news media had been reduced to wartime cheerleaders, and people in this country had largely been shielded from the ugly realities of the war. My aim was to present information difficult to find in the mainstream media, and to explain America's extraordinary predilection to go to war. Ten years later, events compelled me to update the book. The September 11 attacks provided an opportunity for George W. Bush to declare a "War on Terrorism," which in practice turned out to be an endless binge of war-making. The second edition was published in early 2002, following the U.S. invasion of Afghanistan. The Bush Administration then turned to preparing for a new war against Iraq. A thin rhetorical veneer about combating terrorism and the proliferation of weapons of mass destruction hardly concealed its underlying aim: to impose a new U.S. client regime in the Middle East and assure control over a country that has the world's second largest known oil reserves. As the present edition goes to press, the U.S. is occupying Afghanistan and Iraq. In an effort to quell armed resistance, the U.S. military is taking harsh punitive measures against the civilian populations of both countries, feeding a spiral of violence that has repercussions around the world and is placing us all in greater danger.

This book chronicles over two centuries of U.S. foreign wars, beginning with the Indian wars. During this time, America's machinery of war has grown into a behemoth that dominates our economy and society and extends around the globe. Although the Bush Administration has been particularly bellicose, this country's addiction to war began long before Bush came to power and will undoubtedly survive his departure. The costs of this growing addiction are now being felt more acutely at home. Soldiers and their families are paying the heaviest price, but everyone is affected. Skyrocketing military spending is contributing to huge government deficits, causing sharp cuts in domestic programs, including education, health care, housing, public transport, and environmental protection. At the same time, the "War on Terrorism" is being used as an excuse to step up police surveillance and erode our civil liberties. I hope this book will spur reflection and debate about militarism, and encourage creative action to change our direction.

It's impossible to thank all of the people who have contributed to the creation of this book here. Instead, I will mention only three: My mother, Carol Andreas, who introduced me to anti-war activities; my father, Carl Andreas, who first encouraged me to write the book; and Frank Dorrel, whose tireless promotion made a new edition both possible and irresistible.

Joel Andreas, May 2004

Publisher's Note

I first discovered the original 1992 edition of *Addicted to War* about five years ago. I thought it was the best book I had ever read, revealing the true history of U.S. foreign policy and U.S. militarism. I located the author, Joel Andreas (who also illustrated *ATW*), and convinced him to update the book. In April of 2002, I published a new edition with the help of AK Press. The response has been tremendous. Since then, over 180,000 copies have been distributed in the United States and Canada.

Addicted to War is being used as a textbook by hundreds of high school teachers and college professors. Many peace organizations are selling the book at anti-war rallies, teach-ins, and smaller events. It is showing up in schools, churches, and public libraries. More and more bookstores are carrying it. Individuals are ordering multiple copies to give to friends, co-workers, and relatives. I have received thousands of calls, email messages, and letters from people telling me how much they love and appreciate this book!

A Spanish edition of *Addicted to War* is now available in the United States. A Japanese translation has sold over 70,000 copies. Editions in Korean, German, Danish, Thai, Finnish, Indonesian, Italian, Czech, Hungarian, and other languages have also been published. There are plans to make an animated documentary film based on the book. All these versions will help get the book's anti-war message out to greater numbers of people around the world.

I want to thank Joel Andreas for giving us a powerful educational tool that reveals the sad and painful truth about U.S. militarism. We are honored that some of America's most courageous peace educators and activists have endorsed the book. Thanks to Yumi Kikuchi and Gen Morita for their support and for making the Japanese edition of *Addicted to War* possible. Thanks to the *Veterans For Peace* and to the other anti-war organizations listed at the back of the book for using *ATW* to help raise awareness. Thanks to AK Press for co-publishing *ATW* with me. Special thanks to my friends, to my family, and to S. Brian Willson, for supporting this project from the beginning.

Finally, I want to thank you—the reader—for your concern about the issues addressed in this book. I encourage you to use it to help bring about a change of consciousness in this country. Please consider taking a copy to a teacher who might use it in class. Take a copy to your church, synagogue, or mosque. Send one to your congressperson, city council member, or someone in the media. Show it to friends and family. And please also encourage them to listen to or watch *Democracy Now*, hosted by Amy Goodman, which is now on over 375 radio and television stations across the country. I also recommend the website: www.goodfilms.org for excellent anti-war films.

Education is the key. It's up to each of us to do our part. We can make a difference, all of us together. People around the world are counting on us to end our country's addiction to war.

Frank Dorrel, November 2005

The United States maintains the largest and **most powerful military in history**. U.S. warships dominate the oceans, its missiles and bombers can strike targets on every continent, and hundreds of thousands of U.S. troops are stationed overseas. Every few years the U.S. sends soldiers, warships and warplanes to **fight in distant countries**. Many countries go to war, but the U.S. is **unique** in both the **size and power** of its military and its **propensity to use it**.

The **costs** of being a **military superpower** and **waging wars** around the world are **high**. Because hundreds of billions of dollars are funneled to the Pentagon every year, the government skimps on providing for **basic needs** of people here at home. **Cutbacks in social programs** have caused far **more devastation** in this country than any **foreign army** ever has.

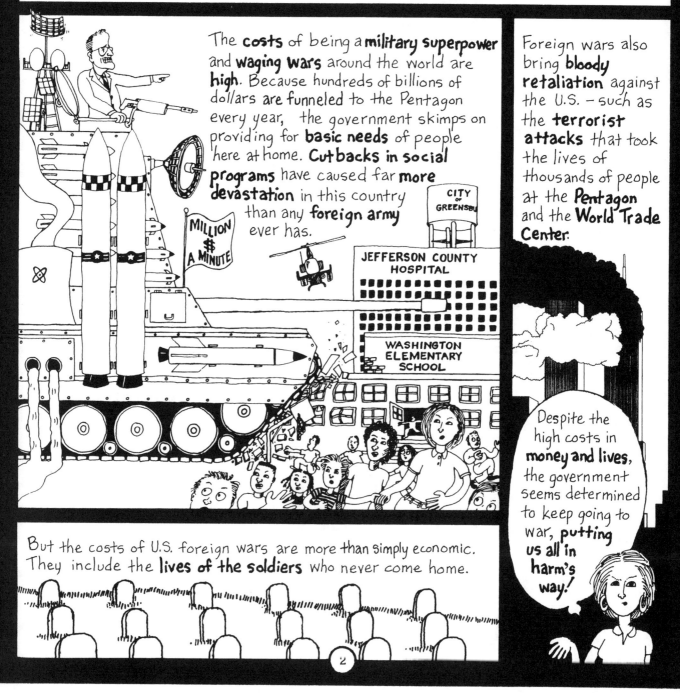

Foreign wars also bring **bloody retaliation** against the U.S. – such as the **terrorist attacks** that took the lives of thousands of people at the **Pentagon** and the **World Trade Center**.

Despite the high costs in **money and lives**, the government seems determined to keep going to war, **putting us all in harm's way!**

But the costs of U.S. foreign wars are more than simply economic. They include the **lives of the soldiers** who never come home.

2

But **why** is the United States always **getting into wars?**

Good question!

I'll have to read up on this...

Two centuries ago, the United States was a collection of **thirteen small colonies** on the Atlantic coast of North America. Today it **dominates the globe** in a way that even the most powerful of past empires could not have imagined.

The path to **world power** has **not** been **peaceful**

Chapter 1
"Manifest Destiny"

The **American revolutionaries** who rose up against **King George** in 1776 spoke eloquently about the **right of every nation to determine its own destiny.**

"When in the course of human events it becomes necessary for one people to **dissolve** the political bands which have connected them with another, and assume, among the **Powers of the earth**, the separate and equal station to which the Laws of Nature and of Nature's God entitle them..."

Thomas Jefferson, from the <u>Declaration of Independence</u>, 1776

Unfortunately, after they won the right to determine **their own destiny** they thought they should determine everyone else's too!

The leaders of the **newly independent colonies** believed that they were preordained to rule all of North America. This was so obvious to them that they called it **"Manifest Destiny."**

"We must march from **ocean to ocean**. ...It is the destiny of the **white race**."

Representative Giles of Maryland

This "manifest destiny" soon led to genocidal wars against the **Native American peoples**. The U.S. Army ruthlessly **seized** their land, driving them west and slaughtering those who resisted.

During the century that followed the American Revolution, the Native American peoples were defeated one by one, their lands were taken, and they were confined to **reservations**. The number of dead has never been counted. But the tragedy did not end with the dead. The Native peoples' **way of life** was devastated.

③

"I can still see the butchered women and children lying heaped and scattered all along the crooked gulch as plain as when I saw them with eyes still young. And I can see that something else died there in the bloody mud, and was buried in the blizzard. A **people's dream** died there. It was a beautiful dream ...the nation's hoop is **broken and scattered.**"

④

Black Elk, spiritual leader of the Lakota people and survivor of the Wounded Knee massacre in South Dakota

By 1848 the United States had seized **nearly half of Mexico's territory.**

United States

Wyoming

Nevada

California

Utah

Colorado

Kansas

Arizona

New Mexico

Oklahoma

Territory Seized from Mexico

Texas

Mexico

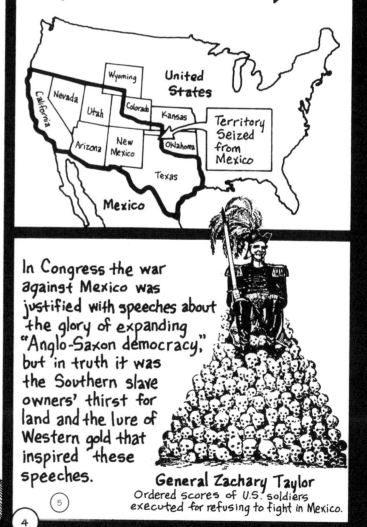

In Congress the war against Mexico was justified with speeches about the glory of expanding "Anglo-Saxon democracy," but in truth it was the Southern slave owners' thirst for land and the lure of Western gold that inspired these speeches.

General Zachary Taylor
Ordered scores of U.S. soldiers executed for refusing to fight in Mexico.

⑤

With their domain now stretching from **coast to coast** the "Manifest Destiny" crowd began to dream of an **overseas empire**. Economic factors drove these ambitions. Col. Charles Denby, a railroad magnate and an ardent **expansionist**, argued: ⑥

"Our condition at home is **forcing** us to commercial expansion... Day by day, **production is exceeding home consumption**... We are after markets, the greatest **markets** in the world."

Calls for **empire** were echoing through the halls of Washington.

"I firmly believe that when any territory outside the **present territorial limits** of the United States becomes necessary for our defense or essential for our commercial development, we ought to **lose no time** in acquiring it."

Senator Orville Platt of Connecticut, 1894 ⑦

To become a world power the U.S. built a **world-class navy**. A gung-ho Theodore Roosevelt was put in charge of it. ⑧

"I should **welcome** almost **any war**, for I think this country **needs one**."

T. Roosevelt, 1897

He didn't have **long** to wait.

The next year, taking a fancy to several Spanish colonies, including **Cuba and the Philippines**, the U.S. declared war on Spain. **Rebel armies** were already fighting for **independence** in both countries and Spain was on the verge of defeat. Washington declared that it was on the rebels' side and Spain quickly capitulated. But the U.S. soon made it clear that it had **no intention of leaving**. ⑨

"The Philippines are **ours forever**... and just beyond the Philippines are China's illimitable markets... the Pacific is **our ocean**."

Senator Albert Beveridge of Indiana, 1900

And for the Senator, the Pacific was **only the beginning**:

"The power that rules the Pacific is the power that **rules the world**... That power is and will forever be the American Republic." ⑩

These colors don't run!

Elaborate **racist theories** were invented to **justify colonialism** and these theories were adopted enthusiastically in Washington. (11)

"We are the **ruling race of the world.** ...We will not renounce our part in the mission of our race, **trustee, under God** of the civilization of the world. ...He has marked us as **his chosen people**... He has made us **adept in government** that we may administer government among **savage and senile peoples.**"

Senator Albert Beveridge, again

But the Filipinos didn't share the views of Senator Beveridge and his buddies.

They fought the new invaders just as they had fought the Spanish. The U.S. subjugated the Philippines with brute force. U.S. soldiers were ordered to "**Burn all and kill all,**" and they did. By the time the Filipinos were defeated, **600,000 had died.** (12)

U.S. soldiers stand on the bones of Filipinos who died in the war

The **Philippines, Puerto Rico,** and **Guam** were made into **U.S. colonies** in 1898. Cuba was formally given its independence, but along with it the Cubans were given the Platt Amendment, which stipulated that the **U.S. Navy** would operate a base in Cuba **forever,** that the U.S. Marines would **intervene at will,** and that Washington would determine Cuba's foreign and financial policies. (13)

Now, don't say I never gave you anything.

Independence

Platt Amendment

During the same period, the U.S. **overthrew Hawaii's Queen Liliuokalani** and transformed these unspoiled Pacific islands into a **U.S. Navy base** surrounded by Dole and Del Monte plantations. In 1903, after Theodore Roosevelt became president, he sent **gun boats** to secure **Panama's** separation from Colombia. The Colombian government had refused Roosevelt's terms for building **a canal**. (14)

If they won't sell, I'll just take it!

Then Uncle Sam began sending his Marines **everywhere**

The Marines went to China, Russia, North Africa, Mexico, Central America, and the Caribbean. (15)

From the Halls of Montezuma to the shores of Tripoli...

Troops march in Siberia during the U.S. invasion of Russia, 1918

Between 1898 and 1934, the Marines invaded Cuba 4 times, Nicaragua 5 times, Honduras 7 times, the Dominican Republic 4 times, Haiti twice, Guatemala once, Panama twice, Mexico 3 times, and Colombia 4 times! (16)

In many countries, the Marines stayed on as an **occupying army**, sometimes for decades. When the Marines finally went home, they typically left the countries they had occupied in the hands of a **friendly dictator**, armed to the teeth to suppress his own people.

"I helped **purify Nicaragua** for the international banking house of Brown Brothers in 1902-1912. I brought light to the **Dominican Republic** for **American sugar interests** in 1916. I helped make **Honduras** right for **American fruit companies** in 1903. In **China** in 1927, I helped see to it that **Standard Oil** went on its way unmolested."

U.S. Marine officer with the head of Silvino Herrera, one of the leaders of Augusto Sandino's rebel army, Nicaragua, 1930

World War I was a horrific battle among the **European colonial powers** over how to **divide up the world**. When President Woodrow Wilson decided to **enter the fray**, he told the American people that he was sending troops to Europe to "**make the world safe for democracy.**"

The Chicago Daily Tribune. FINAL EDITION

U.S. AT WAR: WILSON

U-BOAT SINKS AZTEC, ARMED U.S. STEAMER

NOW FOR THE DEEDS

WARNINGS TO GERMANY!

BOTH HOUSES HASTEN WORK ON PROGRAM

"WE MUST FIGHT FOR JUSTICE AND RIGHTS"

President Tells Joint Session of Congress That German Monarchy Is Threat to All Mankind

But what Wilson was **really after** was what he considered to be the United States' **fair share of the spoils.**

Wilson's ambassador to England said rather forthrightly that the U.S. would declare war on Germany because it was...

(22)

"... the **only way** of maintaining our present **pre-eminent trade status.**"

Ambassador W.H. Page, 1917

For this, **130,274** U.S. soldiers were **sent to their deaths.**

(23)

A horrendous war was concluded with a horrendous event: **200,000 people were killed** instantaneously when the U.S. dropped **nuclear bombs** first on **Hiroshima** and then on **Nagasaki.** Tens of thousands more died later from radiation poisoning.

(26) (27)

"We pray that God might guide us to use [the Bomb] in **His** ways and for **His** purposes."

President Harry Truman, 1945

The defeat of Japan had already been assured **before** the bombs were dropped. Their main purpose was to **demonstrate** to the world the deadly power of America's new **weapon of mass destruction.**

(28)

World War II left the U.S. in a position of **political, economic** and **military superiority.**

(29)

"We must set the pace and assume the responsibility of the **majority stockholder** in this **corporation known as the world.**"

Leo Welch, former Chairman of the Board, Standard Oil of New Jersey (now Exxon) 1946

The U.S. eagerly **assumed responsibility** for determining the economic policies and selecting the management of what it considered to be the **subsidiary companies** that made up the **"corporation known as the world."**

But this didn't go over too well in many nations that considered themselves to be **sovereign countries.**

FUERA YANKIS

Boy, I never read about **any** of that stuff in **here**!

AMERICA Land of Freedom

Chapter 2

The "Cold War" and the Exploits of the Self-Proclaimed "World Policeman"

Go ahead — make my day!

World Cop

The United States, however, had to contend with the **Soviet Union**, which had also emerged from the Second World War as a **world power**. For the next 45 years, the world was caught up in a global turf battle between the "**two superpowers**." The U.S. was always much stronger than its Soviet adversary, but both countries maintained huge military forces to defend and expand their own "**spheres of influence**." The contention between the two powers was called the "**Cold War**" because they never directly engaged each other in battle. But the "Cold War" was marked by plenty of violence in other countries. Typically, the two superpowers lined up on **opposite sides** of every conflict.

USA **USSR**

For its part, the U.S. moved to expand its own "sphere of influence" beyond the Americas and the Pacific to include much of the **old British, French** and **Japanese colonial empires** in **Asia** and **Africa**. In doing so, it had to deal with local aspirations that did not always accord with American plans. To put down insubordination, disorder and disloyalty in its sphere, the new "**majority stockholder**" also appointed itself the "**world policeman**." During the Cold War, Washington **intervened** militarily in foreign countries more than **200 times**.

Don't mess with the U.S.A., buster!

Korea, 1950-1953

After World War II, the **ambitious plans** of the U.S. State Department for Asia and the Pacific were upset completely by **revolutions and anti-colonial wars** from China to Malaysia. A major confrontation developed in **Korea**. Washington decided to intervene directly to show that **Western military technology** could defeat **any Asian army.**

We'll show these #@¿%$!

U.S. warships, bombers, and artillery reduced much of Korea to **rubble.** Over **4,500,000 Koreans died**; three out of four were **civilians. 54,000 U.S. soldiers returned home in coffins.** But the U.S. military, for all of its technological superiority, **did not prevail.** After 3 years of intense warfare, a cease-fire was negotiated. Korea is still divided and some 40,000 U.S. troops remain in southern Korea to this day. ㉛

Waiting for another war.

Dominican Republic, 1965

After a **U.S.-backed military coup,** Dominicans rose up to demand the reinstatement of the overthrown president (who they had elected in a popular vote). Washington, however, was determined to keep its men in power, **no matter who the Dominicans voted for.** 22,000 U.S. troops were sent to suppress the uprising. 3,000 people were **gunned down** in the streets of Santo Domingo. ㉜

YANKEES GO HOME

Vietnam, 1964-1973

For ten years the U.S. assaulted Vietnam with all the deadly force the Pentagon could muster, trying to preserve a **corrupt South Vietnamese regime,** which had been inherited from the **French colonial empire.** The U.S. may have used **more firepower** in Indochina (Vietnam, Laos, and Cambodia) than had been used by **all sides** in all **previous wars** in human history.

Sometimes you have to **destroy** a country to **save** it.

U.S. warplanes dropped **seven million tons** of bombs on Vietnam.

That's the equivalent of one 350-pound bomb **per person!**

Despite the ferocity of the assault on Vietnam, the U.S. was ultimately defeated by a **lightly armed but determined** peasant army.

㉝

400,000 tons of napalm were rained down on the tiny country. **Agent Orange** and other toxic herbicides were used to destroy millions of acres of farmland and forests. Villages were burned to the ground and their residents massacred. Altogether, **two million people died** in the Indochina War, most of them civilians killed by U.S. bombs and bullets. Almost **60,000 U.S. soldiers were killed** and 300,000 wounded.

14

Lebanon, 1982-1983

After the Israeli invasion of Lebanon, the U.S. Marines intervened directly in the **Lebanese civil war**, taking the side of Israel and the right-wing Falange militia.

Which had just massacred 2000 Palestinian civilians.

U.S. Marines marching into Beirut, 1983

241 Marines paid for this intervention with their lives when their barracks were blown up by a **truck bomb.** ㉞

Grenada, 1983

About **110,000 people** live on the tiny Caribbean island of **Grenada.**

About the same number that live in **Peoria, Illinois.**

But, according to **Ronald Reagan**, Grenada represented a ~~threat~~ **to U.S. security.** So he ordered the Pentagon to seize the island and install a new government **more to his liking.** ㉟

"**A lovely** piece of **real estate.**" ㊱

Secretary of State George Schultz, 1983

I'm a Bechtel man and a Pentagon fan

Libya, 1986

Washington loved **King Idris**, the Libyan monarch who happily turned over his country's **oil reserves** to Standard Oil for **next to nothing.** It hates **Col. Qadhafi,** who threw the King out. In 1986, Reagan ordered U.S. warplanes to bomb the Libyan capital, Tripoli, claiming that Qadhafi was responsible for a bomb attack at a German disco that **killed two U.S. soldiers.** It's unlikely that very many of the hundreds of Libyans killed or injured in the U.S. bombing raid **knew anything** about the German bombing.

The nerve of those terrorists —**bombing** those poor people!

㊲

15

So far we've recounted wars that have **involved U.S. troops.**

But there are many **other wars** in which Washington is involved **behind the scenes.**

After World War II, Britain was compelled to dispose of its **colonial empire** in the Middle East. The British gave a big chunk of the land known as **Palestine** to **European Jews** displaced by the **Holocaust.** The problem was that there were already people living there. The result has been five decades of violence and war. Hundreds of thousands of Palestinians were **driven from their homes** in what became Israel. The center of the conflict has been the **West Bank** and **Gaza**, where Palestinians have lived for decades under **Israeli occupation.**

The U.S. provides crucial political support and billions of dollars a year in aid to Israel, including the most **advanced weaponry.** More than three decades of occupation of the West Bank and Gaza have produced bitter anger not only at Israel but also at the United States. As **Palestinian teenagers** continue to die in confrontations with the **Israeli Army** this anger only grows.

Made in USA

38

The U.S. government stands behind its friends - including dictatorial regimes suppressing their own people. In the 1970s and '80s **popular insurgencies** challenged corrupt dictatorships in **Central America.** The Pentagon and the CIA armed and trained security forces and death squads that killed hundreds of thousands of people, mostly **unarmed peasants**, in Nicaragua, El Salvador, and Guatemala.

39

Don't believe them - they were terrorists **disguised as peasants!**

Many of the military officers responsible for the **worst atrocities** in Central America were trained at the Pentagon's **"School of the Americas"** in Georgia. The School trains officers from all over Latin America. Its training manuals recommend **torture** and **summary execution.** Its graduates have returned to establish military regimes and **terrorize** their own people.

CLOSE the **School of Assassins**

NO MORE TORTURE TRAINING

40

Fort Benning is a Terrorist Training Camp

41

Today, bloody U.S.-backed counter-insurgency wars continue in **Colombia, Mexico, Peru,** the **Philippines** and other countries. In Colombia, a corrupt U.S.-backed army fights alongside paramilitary forces that have **slaughtered whole villages** and hundreds of opposition **union leaders** and **politicians.** The U.S. has been getting more deeply involved, under the cover of the **"War on Drugs,"** providing billions of dollars of arms used to continue the killing.

US   US

The CIA and the Pentagon have also organized **proxy armies** to overthrow governments that are **not well-liked in Washington**. In 1961, for instance, U.S. warships ferried **a small army of mercenaries** to Cuba, hoping to reverse the **Cuban Revolution**. They landed at the **Bay of Pigs**.

We'll **show 'em!**

Cubano

It was the **fifth U.S. invasion** of Cuba. But this time the U.S. was **defeated**.

㊷

BOOM

In the 1970s and '80s, the **CIA** was **particularly busy** financing, training and arming **guerrilla armies** around the world

For years the U.S. backed Portugal's efforts to hang on to its **colonies in southern Africa**, helping it stave off independence wars in **Angola** and **Mozambique**.

In 1975, after a democratic revolution in Portugal, the Portuguese **called it quits.**

But Washington didn't!

Instead, it teamed up with the **apartheid regime** in South Africa to supply a **mercenary army** to fight the new government in independent Angola. And in Mozambique, top U.S. and South African politicians and ex-military officers sponsored a **particularly brutal bunch** of mercenaries who massacred tens of thousands of peasants.

㊸

Democracy!

Freedom!

USA

South African Apartheid Regime

And then, of course, there are the "contras."

After the **Nicaraguan people** overthrew the U.S.-backed dictatorship of the Somoza family in 1979, the CIA gathered together the **remnants of Somoza's hated National Guard** and sent them back to Nicaragua with all the weapons they could carry– to **loot, burn, and kill.**

"[The contras are] the **moral equivalent** of our founding fathers."

Ronald Reagan, 1985

I'm a contra too!

44

In 1979, the Soviet Union invaded **Afghanistan** to prop up a friendly regime. **Soviet occupation** met **fierce popular resistance**. The CIA stepped in to arm, finance and train the Afghan **mujahedin guerrillas,** working closely with the Pakistani and Saudi governments. With generous support from Washington and its allies, the mujahedin defeated the Soviets after a **brutal decade-long war.**

45

Among the CIA's collaborators in this war was a Saudi named **Osama bin Laden.** Together with the CIA, bin Laden supplied the Afghan mujahedin with money and guns to fight the Soviets. The Afghan war helped **militarize** an **international Islamic movement** to rid the Muslim world of foreign domination. Ultimately, this movement didn't like the **United States** any more than the **Soviets.** At that time, however, the U.S. backers of bin Laden and the mujahedin were not overly concerned about their wider goals.

46

We will drive **all infidel troops** from Muslim lands!

That's right! Let's whip the **Evil Empire!**

In the 1980s, Reagan **stepped up the arms race**, increasing military spending to unprecedented levels. The Soviets, with a much smaller economy, **struggled to keep up.**

Two can play **this** game!

USA

USSR

But they couldn't. Massive military spending put **tremendous strain** on Soviet society, contributing to its **collapse.** The U.S. **won the arms race** and the **Cold War.**

As the Cold War came to an end, some people began talking about an "**era of world peace**" and a "**peace dividend.**" But behind closed doors at the White House and the Pentagon the talk was quite different.

They were busy planning a **new era of wars**

We're the only **superpower** now!

NEW WORLD ORDER

Chapter 3
The
"New World Order"

In 1989, as the "Eastern Bloc" began to **crumble,** top U.S. government strategists gathered to discuss the **world situation.** The Soviet Union, they happily agreed, was no longer **able or inclined** to counter U.S. military intervention abroad. It was time, they decided, to **demonstrate U.S. military power** to the world. The White House wanted some **decisive victories.**

Much Weaker Enemy.

Much Weaker Enemy

Yes!

Yes!

Yes!

"In cases where the U.S. confronts **much weaker enemies,** our challenge will be not simply to defeat them, but to defeat them **decisively and rapidly.**"

From a National Security Council policy review document, 1989

47

Panama, 1989

Panama was the first country selected to be the "much weaker enemy."

Ever since **U.S. warships** brought Panama into existence, U.S. troops have intervened in the small country whenever Washington deemed it necessary. **George H.W. Bush** continued this **tradition** in 1989, sending in **25,000 troops.**

Supposedly to arrest a drug dealer.

The drug charges were only a pretext. The real motive was assuring U.S. control over the **Panama Canal** and the extensive **U.S. military bases** in that country. A **new Panamanian president** was sworn in at a U.S. air base moments before the invasion. Hardly "Mr. Clean," the man the U.S. State Department picked for the job, Guillermo Endara, ran a bank that is notorious for **money laundering.**

(48)

We believe in **free enterprise!**

Of course, not only Panamanian banks are involved in this business. Most **big U.S. banks** have set up branches in Panama City.

(49)

Gotta get a piece of the action!

And drug trafficking and money laundering have **increased** sharply in Panama since "Operation Just Cause."

(50)

Aduana/ Customs

Cocaine

According to Panamanian human rights groups, **several thousand people were killed** in the U.S. invasion. 26 were U.S. soldiers. 50 were Panamanian soldiers. The rest were **civilians**, cut down by the overwhelming U.S. firepower poured into **crowded neighborhoods** in poor sections of Panama City and Colón. (51)

Many of the dead were put in **garbage bags** and **secretly buried** in mass graves.

Iraq, 1991

Only 13 months after the invasion of Panama, the U.S. went to war again — this time on a much **larger scale**. The 1991 U.S.-Iraq War continued an **epic battle** for control over the **immensely rich oil fields** of the Persian Gulf that began over 75 years earlier.

During World War I, the British conquered the region that is now Iraq and Kuwait, **seizing** it from the **declining Ottoman Empire**.

We didn't **conquer** the Arabs — we **liberated** them!

(52) In 1920 hundreds of British soldiers and many more Iraqis died when the British Army suppressed a **revolt** against **British rule**. Britain ended up installing a **hand-picked "King of Iraq."** The new monarch promptly signed a deal with British and American oil companies giving them the right to **exploit all of Iraq's oil** for 75 years in exchange for a pittance in royalties.

God save the **King**!

As the British Empire declined, the U.S. became the **senior partner** in an enduring **Anglo-American alliance**. The Middle East became a key part of their global "sphere of influence."

The Middle East possesses almost **two-thirds** of the **world's known oil reserves.** Control over the flow of oil by U.S. and British companies gave Washington **strategic power** over Europe, Japan and the developing world. The U.S. State Department declared that Middle Eastern oil was...

(53)

"...a stupendous source of **strategic power**... one of the **greatest prizes** in world history"

Washington came to think of the oil fields in the Middle East as its own **private reserves.**

(54)

What are you up to?

Exploring to see if there are any **vital American interests** under your soil

Mobil

In 1958, U.S. and British oil companies were startled when the **King of Iraq** was **overthrown.** The new leader, a nationalist military officer named Abdel Karim Qasim, demanded changes in the **sweetheart deals** the monarchy had made with the oil companies. He also helped form **OPEC**, the cartel of oil producing countries.

Besides, the guy was consorting with communists!

CIA

In 1963, the **CIA** collaborated with the **Ba'ath Party** to **murder** Qasim and overthrow his government. The Ba'ath Party was also nationalist but at least it was **anti-communist.** It systematically killed its Leftist opponents and the CIA was **happy to help.**

These Ba'ath guys are **efficient.** We give them lists of suspected communists and they get the **job done!**

(55)

CIA

Among the CIA's collaborators in the 1963 coup was a young military officer named **Saddam Hussein**, who later emerged as the top leader in Iraq.

Despite U.S. support, Saddam Hussein failed to seize any of Iran's oilfields, so he then turned his attention to the **oilfields** of his **southern neighbor**.

I decided to **invade Kuwait!**

Hussein apparently expected that the U.S. would also tacitly go along with his invasion of Kuwait. For the U.S., however, Kuwait was **very different** from Iran. The **Kuwaiti emir** was a **loyal friend** of the U.S. and British oil companies and a close political ally of the United States. George H.W. Bush worried that the huge Iraqi army had become a threat to U.S. domination of the Middle East.

"Our jobs, **our way of life**, our own freedom, and the freedom of friendly countries around the world would all suffer if **control** of the **world's great oil reserves** fell into the hands of Saddam Hussein"

George H.W. Bush, August 1990

Bush decided Hussein had to be **punished** for trespassing on an **oil-rich U.S. protectorate**.

The Honorable George H.W. Bush, December 1990

"**He's going to get his ass kicked!**"

The war had a **message** for the world:

The Pentagon launched the **most intensive bombing campaign** in history using conventional bombs, **cluster bombs** (designed to rip bodies apart), **napalm** and **phosphorous** (which cling to and burn skin), and **fuel-air** explosives (which have the impact of small nuclear bombs). Later, the U.S. used munitions tipped with **depleted uranium**, which is now suspected as a cause of **cancer** among both Iraqis and U.S. soldiers and their children. Iraq was bombed back to a **pre-industrial age** and tens of thousands were killed.

Nuke Baghdad!

"What we say goes!"

AMERICA IS NO. 1 —AND DON'T YOU FORGET IT!

George H.W. Bush, February 1991

Baghdad and Basra were **bombed relentlessly,** killing thousands of civilians.

(64)

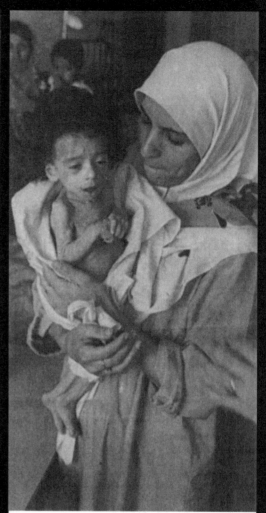

Iraq had already begun to withdraw from Kuwait when Bush launched the ground war. The main aim of the ground offensive was, in fact, **not** to drive the Iraqi troops out of Kuwait, but to **keep them from leaving.** The **"gate was closed"** and tens of thousands of soldiers, who were trying to go home, were **systematically slaughtered.** Elsewhere, U.S. tanks and bulldozers intentionally **buried thousands of soldiers alive** in their trenches in a tactic designed mainly to "destroy Iraqi defenders."

(65)

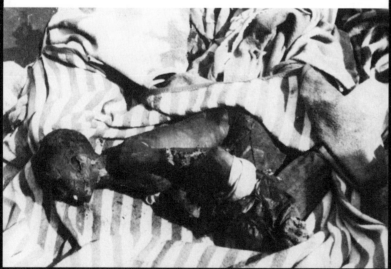

"In the life of a nation there comes a moment when we are called upon to define **who we are** and **what we believe."**

George H. Bush
January 1991

(66)

Tens of thousands of Iraqis died during the war. And the tragedy continued after the war ended. Even more people died from **water-borne diseases** that spread because the U.S. systematically destroyed Iraq's **electrical, sewage treatment** and **water treatment** systems.

For over a decade, the U.S. insisted on maintaining the most **severe economic sanctions** regime in history, continuing to strangle the devastated Iraqi economy, with dire consequences for the Iraqi people.

(67)

In 1999, **UNICEF** estimated that **infant and child mortality** had more than doubled since the war. It attributed this sharp increase in mortality mainly to malnutrition and deteriorating health conditions caused by the **war** and **ongoing sanctions**. It estimated that **half a million more children died** as a result. That's 5,200 children a month. ⑥⑧

That ought to **teach Saddam a lesson** he won't soon forget!

Have a Nice War

Bush's sucessor, Bill Clinton, not only kept up the **sanctions**, but also continued to **bomb Iraq** regularly for **8 years**.

And the U.S. war on Iraq was **far from over**

Kosovo, 1999

In the late 1990s, after enduring **years of abuse** at the hands of a Serbian-dominated Yugoslav government, Albanian rebels in Kosovo started a **war for secession**. The U.S. usually does not support minority groups demanding separation. But it **all depends** on whether the U.S. supports the government of the country facing dismemberment. For instance, the U.S. supports **Kurdish separatists** in **Iraq and Iran**, but across the border in **Turkey**, a close ally, Washington has provided tons of arms to **crush the Kurds**. With U.S. help, tens of thousands have been killed. ⑥⑨

Our policy is clear— We support people **fighting** for their **freedom** and oppose **terrorist separatists**

US   US

Because the **Yugoslav strongman**, Slobodan Milosevic, was being less than cooperative with U.S. efforts to extend its influence in Eastern Europe, **breaking up Yugoslavia** was a cause the U.S. could warm up to. The Clinton Administration embraced the Kosovo Liberation Army, despite their **drug dealing, ethnic extremism** and **brutality**. Following established practice, the Administration issued an ultimatum the Yugoslavs **could not possibly accept**. ⑦⓪

Here's the deal. First, **NATO** takes over Kosovo. Second, **NATO** has free access to all of Yugoslavia. Third, you help pay for the **NATO-run** government. **Sign here or we bomb you.**

The NATO bombing turned an ugly but small-scale Yugoslav counter-insurgency operation into a massive **ethnic cleansing** drive. After the bombing began, Serbian soldiers and militia members began driving hundreds of thousands of Albanians out of the country and killed thousands of others. When the **Albanians** returned under NATO protection, **Serbian** and **Gypsy** residents were driven out and killed. Ultimately, the war served **U.S. political objectives**, while causing tremendous death and suffering on all sides and greatly **aggravating ethnic antagonisms**. ⑦①

Chapter 4
The
"War on Terrorism"

After the horrific **September 11 terrorist attacks** on the World Trade Center and the Pentagon, **one question** was so **sensitive** it was seldom seriously addressed by the U.S. news media.

To find out, it makes sense to ask the **prime suspect** himself. As U.S. warplanes began bombing Afghanistan, **Osama bin Laden** released a videotaped message. He **praised** the **September 11 attacks** and called for more attacks on the United States. Then he spelled out his **motivations** quite clearly.

Mom, **why** did they **do it?**

"What America is tasting now is something insignificant compared to what we have tasted for scores of years. Our nation (the Islamic world) has been tasting this **humiliation** and **degradation** for more than **80 years**. Its sons are killed, its **blood is shed**, its sanctuaries are attacked and no one hears and no one heeds. Millions of innocent children are being killed as I speak. They are being killed in **Iraq** without committing any sins.... To **America**, I say only a few words to it and its people. I swear to God, who has elevated the skies without pillars, **neither America nor the people** who live in it will **dream of security** before we live it here in **Palestine** and not before all the **infidel armies leave the land of Muhammad**, peace be upon him." [72]

Osama bin Laden
Oct. 7, 2001

Few people anywhere in the world, including the Middle East, support bin Laden's terrorist methods. But most people in the Middle East **share his anger** at the United States. They are angry at the U.S. for supporting **corrupt** and **dictatorial regimes** in the region, for **supporting Israel** at the expense of the Palestinians and for imposing **U.S. dictates** on the Middle East through **military might** and **brutal economic sanctions**.

The Bush Administration immediately instructed U.S. television networks to "**exercise caution**" in airing bin Laden's taped messages. The official reason?

The tapes may contain **secret coded messages** for terrorist operatives

But were **covert messages** the Administration's main concern? Perhaps it was more worried about the impact of bin Laden's **overt message** – that the **September 11** attacks were carried out in **retaliation** for U.S. foreign policy and particularly **U.S. military intervention** in the Middle East.

If Americans realized that U.S. military intervention abroad brought retaliation – causing **death and destruction at home** – we might **think twice** about whether the U.S. should be so **eager to go to war** overseas

The Pentagon has demonstrated time and again that its advanced weaponry can **devastate countries** targeted for attack, **leveling** basic **infrastructure** and **killing thousands**, even hundreds of thousands of people.

It would be **naive** to think there would be **no retaliation**

Over the last several decades the **true costs** of the wars the U.S. has waged overseas have been largely **hidden**. We have had to **pay the military bills** but few Americans have died. The **death** and **destruction** were all **overseas**. That changed on **September 11**.

> The **violence reached the United States**

The September 11 attacks, however, were not simply acts of **retribution**. They were also **provocation**. Bin Laden expected the U.S. to respond with **massive violence**, knowing this would bring him **new recruits**. Ultimately, he hoped to win the majority of the Muslim world to support his **holy war on the U.S.**

> More **martyrs**, more **recruits!**

The Bush Administration responded according to **bin Laden's script**. George W. Bush declared a **"War on Terrorism,"** using "good vs. evil" rhetoric that mirrored bin Laden's. Bush and his advisors were ready - **even eager** - for the war bin Laden wanted. They saw the September 11 attacks as a **grand opportunity** to boost military spending and demonstrate U.S. military power to the world.

73

> "This will be a monumental struggle of **good versus evil**... This **crusade**, this **war on terrorism**, is going to take a while"

George W. Bush
September 12 and 16, 2001

The self-righteous **"good vs. evil"** rhetoric of the "War on Terrorism" sharpens ironies that have long shadowed U.S. pronouncements against **state-sponsored terrorism**. President Bush, for instance, promised to scour the globe in search of **states** that **harbor terrorists**.

> He could have started in the **State of Florida**

> What do you mean?

For over forty years, **Miami** has served as the base of operations for well-financed groups of **Cuban exiles** that have carried out violent **terrorist attacks on Cuba**.

> Most recently, they **bombed** a number of Havana tourist spots in 1997, killing an Italian tourist, and they tried to **assassinate** Fidel Castro in Panama in 2000.

29

It would not be difficult for the U.S. government to find evidence involving these terrorist organizations because the **CIA** and the **Pentagon trained** many of their **members**. Take, for instance, **Luis Posada Carriles** and **Orlando Bosch**, suspected masterminds of the **bombing** of a **Cuban passenger airliner** that claimed the lives of **73 people**. ⑦④

"All of Castro's planes are **warplanes**"

Orlando Bosch, 1987, defending the bombing of the civilian Cuban plane

Before Posada Carriles could be tried for the airline bombing, he **escaped** from a **prison** in Venezuela and found a job **supplying arms** to the CIA-backed **Nicaraguan Contras**.

My **experience** in the **CIA** gave me the **right credentials** for the job ⑦⑤

Posada's accomplice, Orlando Bosch, has long been **protected from extradition** by the U.S. government. Although Bosch was convicted of carrying out a **bazooka attack** on a ship in **Miami harbor**, President George H.W. Bush – at the urging of his son Jeb – prevented his expulsion from the country. Bush signed an **executive pardon** providing Bosch with **safe haven** in Florida. Bosch promised to...

"Rejoin **the struggle!**" ⑦⑥ ⑦⑦

Hold on! Let me set the record straight. I **pardon only freedom fighters**, not terrorists!

If George W. Bush had been serious about going after **all** states that **harbor terrorists**, he would have issued an **ultimatum** to **his brother**, the governor of Florida.

Listen Jeb, you're going to have to **cough up** the terrorists or we start **bombing Miami** tomorrow!

Posada, Bosch and their friends are **only a few** of the violent characters whose activities have been sponsored by the CIA. Many of the CIA's "**covert operations**" – bombings, **assassinations, sabotage,** and **paramilitary massacres** – are terrorism by any definition. Many of the shadowy figures involved in these activities are still working with the CIA around the world. But others – including **Osama bin Laden** – have turned on their former American partners. ⑦⑧

It's **too bad.** They made such a **good team.**

Afghanistan, 2001 - ?

Bush's **"War on Terrorism"** began with U.S. warplanes **bombing Afghanistan**, the unfortunate country where bin Laden chose to locate his headquarters. At that time, Afghanistan was ruled by fundamentalist Muslim clerics of the Taliban movement, whom both bin Laden and the CIA had supported during the anti-Soviet war. Now, Washington decided to **destroy its former allies**.

> The people of Afghanistan suffered the consequences

U.S. bombs killed hundreds – and perhaps thousands – of civilians, and the war cut off relief supplies to millions already **facing starvation**. The total number of deaths will never be known, but it's certain that many more **civilians died** in the U.S. assault on Afghanistan than in the attack on the World Trade Center. ⑦⑨

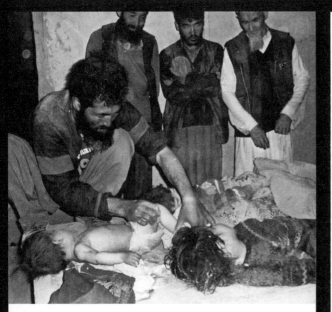

Relatives prepare four children for burial after a U.S. air strike in Kabul, October 2001

The U.S. made common cause with a new set of Afghan allies - **brutal regional warlords**. Under U.S. auspices, Islamic fundamentalism has been replaced by **brazen corruption** as warlords fight for power and prey on the people under their jurisdiction. The **opium trade**, which the zealous Taliban clerics had briefly suppressed, once again flourishes under the warlords. ⑧⓪

> And Afghanistan regained its place as the **world's top opium producer**

Iraq, 2003 - ?

From the day they took office, Bush and his key lieutenants **set their sights on Iraq**. After 9-11, they packaged an invasion as part of the "War on Terrorism." To win U.N. backing, they claimed Saddam Hussein was developing **nuclear, chemical, and biological weapons**. The threat was so **imminent**, they said, that an immediate invasion was **imperative**.

> "We can't **wait** for the final proof - the smoking gun – that could come in the form of a **mushroom cloud**"

George W. Bush
October 2002 ⑧①

We now know that Iraq had no "weapons of mass destruction" and that the Bush Administration **manipulated evidence** to justify its war plans. Even then, it was clear that the specter of such weapons was just a pretext. The U.S. made no secret of its underlying **war aims** – to install a **pro-U.S. regime** in Iraq and increase U.S. military and political power in the Middle East. Bush, therefore, had little use for U.N. weapons inspectors in Iraq.

Get those *%&# inspectors out of the way– I'm getting ready to **bomb the place!**

82

The U.N. **refused to endorse** the invasion, but the U.S. and Britain went ahead anyway. The Iraqi army was **decimated** and thousands of civilians who were unlucky enough to get in the way were also killed.

83

As soon as U.S. troops captured Baghdad, elated American officials began **issuing threats** to Iraq's neighbors, Syria and Iran. The message was: Go along with the American program **or else...**

84

"This doesn't mean, **necessarily**, that other governments have to fall. They can **moderate their behavior**"

Senior U.S. official, April 2003

The Bush Administration had **big plans**. Based on Iraq's **tremendous oil wealth** and **U.S. military might**, American officials hoped to create a client regime in Iraq and use it as a **base of U.S. power** in the heart of the Arab Middle East. They brought in a group of **émigré politicians**, intending to install them as leaders of a new government. Their **favorite** was Ahmed Chalabi, a wealthy businessman who was convicted of bank fraud in Jordan.

Don't sweat it buddy– we all get accused of **financial malfeasance** now and then

85

Chalabi won the hearts of White House officials in part by declaring that he favored pulling Iraq out of OPEC, and then **privatizing Iraqi oil** and selling it off to foreign companies.

"American companies have a **big shot** at Iraqi oil"

Ahmed Chalabi
Sept. 2002

86

Because the U.S. is **extremely unpopular** among Arabs throughout the Middle East, if Iraqis actually were allowed to vote freely, they could hardly be expected to elect pro-U.S. candidates. That's why the U.S. adamantly **resisted holding popular elections** in occupied Iraq, instead proposing that members of a new governing assembly be selected by handpicked "caucuses."

89

"In a post-war situation like this, if you start holding elections, the people who are **rejectionists** tend to win"

Paul Bremer, head of the Coalition Provisional Authority, June 2003

By "rejectionists" Bremer meant those who oppose U.S. occupation

100,000 Iraqis march to demand popular elections, Baghdad, January 19, 2004

The U.S. occupation authority in Iraq was hardly a model of democratic government. Newspapers and radio and television stations that criticized the authority were **shut down**.

They displayed a blatant **lack of appreciation** for their liberators!

Tens of thousands of Iraqis **disappeared** into prisons run by the U.S. military. Prisoners were held without charge and were subjected to **humiliation**, **sexual abuse**, and **torture**.

90

"Now all Iraqis can **taste liberty** in their native land!"

91

U.S. Attorney General John Ashcroft after he sent a team to rebuild Iraq's system of courts and prisons in 2003

Facing a **hostile population**, the U.S. military policed Iraqi cities and villages with a **heavy hand**. Scores of Iraqis were killed as they protested against the occupation. **Journalists** were gunned down as they covered U.S. military operations. Others – who were simply in the wrong place at the wrong time – were **shot at military checkpoints** or when soldiers raided their neighborhoods.

The U.S. occupation of Iraq followed the familiar path of previous **colonial adventures**. Iraqis organized **armed resistance** and the U.S. military took increasingly harsh **punitive measures** against the population, inspiring **fear** and **indignation**. (92)

As resistance grew, American commanders became increasingly **frustrated** and **aggressive**. After four U.S. military contractors were brutally killed in Falluja, the U.S. took **revenge**. Hundreds of residents were killed as densely-packed neighborhoods were **shelled** by tanks and **bombed** and **strafed** by warplanes and helicopters. The siege of Falluja only incited **wider opposition** throughout Iraq to U.S. occupation.

(94)

As U.S. soldiers and Iraqis died in daily battles, Bush's response was swaggering **cowboy rhetoric**.

"There are some who feel like... they can attack us there. My answer is — **bring them on!**"

George W. Bush, Washington, DC July 2003

(93)

I wonder **if he'd like to** do guard duty here in Baghdad

By spring 2004, it was clear that Bush's **grandiose plans** had **collapsed**. The vast majority of Iraqis **wanted the U.S. out**, and they **wanted nothing to do** with any politicians associated with Washington.

"**They** don't want us here and **we** don't want to be here"

Unidentified American soldier in Baghdad

(95)

The U.S. occupation of Afghanistan and Iraq, together with continued U.S. support for the Israeli occupation of Palestine, have **added fuel** to **simmering anti-American sentiments** across the Middle East.

Resistance drove up the costs of occupation. Keeping over **135,000 troops** in Iraq cost over one **billion dollars a week**. Every day U.S. soldiers **returned home in coffins** or disabled for life. But politicians and generals in Washington continued to insist that they would **never back down**, no matter what the cost. ⒐⒍

Our **credibility** as a military superpower is **on the line** now!

By invading and occupying Muslim countries, the U.S. is only **inviting more attacks** on U.S. soldiers and other American targets. The Pentagon has promised to respond with more violence.

"We will **export death and violence** to the four corners of the earth in defense of our great nation!"

U.S. special forces officer, Afghanistan, February 2002 ⒐⒎

The **spiral of bloodshed** is escalating dangerously. America's long-time **addiction to war** has reached a **new level**, creating greater dangers for people in this country and around the world.

Unfortunately, there are some people who **profit handsomely** from this addiction...

For **most** people, the huge Pentagon budget means **less money** in their pockets.

IRS

PENTAGON

But for **some** people, just the **opposite** is true.

War Profits

Over 100,000 companies feed at the Pentagon trough. But the **big money** goes to a handful of huge corporations.

Outa the way! I was here first!

1999 Pentagon Contracts

(98)

United Technolog $2.4 billion

TEXTRON $1.4 billion

NORTHROP GRUMMAN $3.2 billion

BOEING $11.6 billion

Raytheon $6.4 billion

GE $1.7 billion

GENERAL DYNAMICS $4.6 billion

LOCKHEED MARTIN $12.7 billion

TRW $1.4 billion

As they watch **missiles flying** and the **bombs dropping** in the Middle East, top executives of the big weapons manufacturers are adding up their profits, their brains working like **cash registers gone haywire.**

ch-ching

ch-ching

For weapons makers, wars mean more orders – not only from the Pentagon, but also from overseas. After the first Gulf War demonstrated that their weapons can truly **kill on a massive scale,** foreign sales by U.S. weapons manufacturers **skyrocketed.**

(99)

We've got a **real deal** on F-16's this week – buy 100 and **we'll throw in** 1,000 cases of **napalm free!**

FREE NAPALM OFFER! We overstocked! Gulf tested! Gulf proven! Kill like you never have before!

Our weapons kill:
• more
• better
• faster

Who are the war profiteers?

Let's take a look at some of the men in Washington who are most **gung ho** about war...

Dick Cheney

Few politicians can match Dick Cheney's **enthusiasm for war** - or his record of **wanton destruction**. As George H.W. Bush's Secretary of Defense he presided over wars against Panama and Iraq, and then as Vice President under George W. Bush, he led the war drives against Afghanistan and Iraq.

Between wars, Dick has turned his attention from **destruction** to **construction** - that is post-war reconstruction. In 1995, he was named CEO of **Halliburton**, the world's largest oil services company and a major military contractor. After the first Gulf War, Halliburton was hired to help rebuild the Kuwaiti oil industry. Then after the second Gulf War, the company was back to **clean up the mess again** - for a **healthy fee**. ⑩⓪

You've gotta hand it to Dick. He's got an **innovative business strategy** - first bomb it, then clean it up, then bomb it again, then clean it up again!

Halliburton

Halliburton is raking in hundreds of millions of dollars for feeding and housing U.S. troops in Iraq and it got the biggest post-war reconstruction prize - a **secret no-bid contract** to rebuild Iraqi oil facilities that will likely be worth billions. ⑩①

It's **nice** to have friends in Washington!

As Halliburton's CEO, Cheney was **rewarded handsomely**, pocketing millions in salary and stock options every year. He ended up as Halliburton's largest individual stockholder, with a $45 million stake. ⑩②

I **earned** every penny of it!

Cheney got **draft deferments** five times to avoid fighting in Vietnam. But he's eager to send **others** to **fight and die**, and then **reap the benefits**. He's served on the boards of several huge war contractors, and his wife - Lynne - joined the board of Lockheed Martin. After Cheney returned to the White House in 2001, Lockheed got the **biggest plum** in Pentagon history - a contract worth hundreds of billions to make the next generation of fighter jets.

We're just doing our **patriotic duty!**

⑩③

In fact, under the banner of funding the "War on Terrorism," Congress has **abandoned** efforts to avoid budget deficits. Instead, every year it gives the Pentagon what amounts to a **blank check.**

For **whatever** it takes...

PAY TO THE ORDER OF _PENTAGON_ $____
_____ DOLLARS
U.S. Congress

After the end of the **Cold War**, many in Washington were reconsidering the **humongous size** of the military budget, which had converted the U.S. from the world's biggest lender into the **world's biggest debtor.**

USA

Bonds, anyone? T-bills?

Ouch! That **hurts!**

USA

In an effort to balance the federal budget, politicians were beginning to **trim** the Pentagon's **toenails.**

USA

After September 11 all this changed. Bush and the Congress started to pump up the Pentagon's **bloated budget** without restraint.

USA

$

Even Congressional opposition to the far-fetched "missile defense program" collapsed.

Beep Beep

Missile defense, like the "War on Terrorism," **promises to protect Americans** from danger while actually creating a much **more dangerous world.** If other countries think there is any chance the U.S. could block their missiles, they will feel **vulnerable** to U.S. attack. China has already promised to build more and better missiles which could overwhelm the U.S. "missile shield." This will spur a **nuclear arms race in Asia.**

If **China** builds more nuclear missiles, then **India** will. If India does, then **Pakistan** will. If Pakistan...

In 1972, the U.S. and the U.S.S.R. signed the **ABM Treaty** to try to avoid this kind of arms race. In order to pursue missile defense, the U.S. **unilaterally scrapped** the treaty. But that didn't bother missile defense proponents.

107

Hey, the world's changed. **We can win an arms race** with anyone!

In this spirit, Congress **rejected** the **nuclear test ban treaty** (which has been signed by 164 countries) and it continues to finance nuclear weapons research and production. In fact, the Pentagon is eager to develop a new arsenal of small "**battlefield**" nuclear weapons.

108

The U.S. is keeping enough nuclear firepower to **wipe out** most of **humanity.**

Just to be safe!

As potential nuclear targets in Russia have declined, the Pentagon has been retargeting its missiles at "**every reasonable adversary.**"

Which makes other countries feel like they better **hurry up** and get nuclear weapons themselves

42

109

Chapter 6

The High Price of Militarism

Maintaining this huge military machine is **not cheap**. Every year the U.S. spends **hundreds of billions** of dollars on the military. (113)

This figure does not include tens of billions spent on the military occupations of Afghanistan and Iraq

$399,000,000,000 **military budget** 2004 fiscal year

$308 billion 2001

$351 billion 2002

$396 billion 2003

$470 billion (proposed) 2007

Since 1948 the U.S. has spent more than **$15 trillion** to build up its military might. Just **how much** is $15,000,000,000,000 **worth**? (114)

Lemme see...

My God!

It adds up to **more than** the cumulative monetary value of **all human-made wealth** in the U.S.! (115)

In other words, the government has spent more on the military over the last four decades than the value of **all the factories**, machinery, roads, **bridges**, water and sewage systems, **airports**, railroads, **power plants**, office buildings, shopping centers, **schools**, hospitals, hotels, **houses**, etc., in this country **put together!**

Wow!

44

Schools are run-down and over-crowded. In some inner-city high schools, 80% of the students drop out. More than a fifth of all adults **can't read** a job application or a street sign. Yet federal education funding per student has declined substantially over the last two decades.

(120)

We believe in **bake** sale financing.

Skyrocketing prices are causing a crisis in health care. **43 million** people have **no insurance** and millions more have inadequate insurance. More and more people don't get the medical care they need because they can't afford it. Yet **public hospitals are being closed** and the government has failed to enact any serious health care reform.

(121)

INSURED PATIENTS ➡

UNINSURED PATIENTS ⬅

EXIT

Reception

Mom, it hurts!

One-fifth of all **expectant mothers** do not receive **pre-natal care**. This is one reason the U.S. has the highest infant mortality rate in the developed world (twice as high as Japan's). **Every 50 minutes**, a child in the U.S. dies as a result of **poverty or hunger**. Yet Congress has been exceedingly stingy in funding maternal and child health programs.

(122)

I just **love** babies!

Why don't you put your **money** where your **mouth** is, mister?

Yuck!

Vote for Me!

With **rents rising** and **wages falling**, millions of families are living on the verge of eviction. Millions of people end up **living on the streets** Yet when it comes to funding for housing and homelessness, most of Washington seems to have adopted Reagan's attitude.

(123)

Those people **want** to live on the streets!

The administrators who run the nuclear weapons plants have **knowingly** subjected the people who work in them and the people who live near them to **deadly radioactive contamination** — without telling them a word about it.

The government now estimates it will take **25,000 workers** at least **30 years** to clean up the mess at these plants — at a cost of **$300 billion** or more. (130)

And guess who's **paying the bill!**

Beep Beep

What's more, nuclear weapons tests have spread deadly **plutonium** across large tracts of the Southwest and the South Pacific. Many of the 458,000 U.S. soldiers who participated in the atomic testing program are now **dying of cancer.** (131)

Don't worry, kid. It's perfectly safe. Just wear these **goggles!**

?

U.S. ARMY   PVT. GRUNT

But they're not the only ones. **High cancer rates** plague the general population in the testing areas. One study estimated that previous nuclear testing would eventually cause at least **430,000 people** to die of cancer worldwide. (132)

And plutonium remains **highly radioactive** for hundreds of thousands of years.

49

Meanwhile, at military bases around the country they've been **dumping hundreds of thousands of tons of toxic wastes**, including chemical warfare agents, napalm, explosives, PCB's, and heavy metals, creating malignant lagoons and **contaminating the groundwater** of surrounding communities.

There are 11,000 military dump sites that need to be cleaned up. The estimated cost — **$100 to $200 billion**. (133)

I say let's fence 'em all off and call them **national security sacrifice zones.**

DANGE KEEP OU TOXIC W

He's serious — that's what some people are proposing

Another cost of foreign wars is the **retaliation** they bring.

If we weren't always **bombing other people,** we wouldn't have to worry so much about people **bombing us!**

On the eve of the U.S. invasion of Iraq, Homeland Security Secretary Tom Ridge admitted that the war would spur **more terrorist attacks** against the U.S. (134)

" I think we can anticipate... **more threats** because of a potential invasion. I mean it's **fairly predictable.**"

Tom Ridge, March 2003

In other words, the Bush Administration knew that invading Iraq would bring retaliation, but it decided to go ahead and **place us in greater danger** anyway!

The "War on Terrorism" opened a new chapter in U.S. foreign wars, a chapter that may be marked by an **endless cycle of violence.** Some in Washington seem to **relish the prospect.** Emerging from his secret bunker several weeks after the September 11, 2001 attacks, Dick Cheney predicted that the "War on Terrorism" would go on for a long time. (135)

CHENEY

" It may **never end.** At least not in our lifetime"

Cheney, Oct. 2001

As part of this **endless war**, he declared, we have to be prepared for **ongoing terrorist attacks**.

"For the first time in our history we will probably suffer **more casualties** here **at home** than will our troops overseas"

Dick Cheney, October 2001

136

As a result, Cheney warned, we'll have to get used to **invasive security measures**.

137

"We're going to have to take steps... that'll become a **permanent** part of our **way of life**"

Dick Cheney, October 2001

Which brings us to **another cost** of militarism— the **loss of our civil liberties**.

We **never said** this war was not going to have **costs!**

As the United States **barricades itself against the world**, we all suffer the inconveniences of increased security measures. But some of these measures are not simply inconvenient— they are **dangerous**.

Grrrr

FBI

"Homeland security" has become a slogan for eliminating civil rights protections long deemed inconvenient by the **FBI** and other **police agencies**.

Agencies that often give priority to **suppressing political opponents**

In the name of "Homeland security"...

You can now be **jailed indefinitely** without trial.

The police and the FBI – and even the CIA – can more easily **spy on you,** reading your mail and e-mail, listening in on your phone, and breaking into your home.

Thousands of immigrants have been **called in for questioning** simply because they came from predominantly Muslim countries. (138)

Many have been jailed for long periods on **baseless suspicions**

Nearly everyone in this country pays a high price for militarism. But those among us who have paid the **highest price** are the **millions of soldiers** who have been sent overseas to fight.

More than **100,000 U.S. soldiers and sailors have died** in foreign wars since U.S. troops were sent to Korea in 1950. (139)

Hundreds of thousands more have been wounded, many **disabled for life.** Many Gulf War veterans are suffering the effects of **"Gulf War Syndrome."**

Those who survive continue to be **haunted by the wars** they fought in. Half a million **veterans** of the Vietnam War suffer from post-traumatic stress disorder - caused by memories of the horrors of the war. The number of Vietnam vets who have **killed themselves** since the war is greater than the number of U.S. soldiers who died in the war. (140)

Hundreds of thousands of military veterans have ended up living on the streets. (141)

And the **killing goes on**, even between wars.

Every year, more than a thousand U.S. soldiers and sailors are killed in **military accidents**. They are burned to death in fires at sea, crushed by tanks, and blown up by practice artillery fire.

BOOM

U.S. NAVY

They break their necks jumping out of planes in high wind, and crash in **unsafe helicopters**.

SNAP

?!

(142)

These are all victims of Washington's **addiction to militarism**. And there are more victims...

Every year, hundreds of active-duty soldiers and sailors **commit suicide.**

Of course, nobody is **born** with a desire to be **humiliated** and **treated like a "grunt"**; much less to be killed. So **indoctrination** into the culture of militarism starts early.

Bang! Bang! You're dead!

Why do all the networks sound the same? Why are they all **consumed by war fever** every time the White House decides to send troops overseas?

Maybe it's got something to do with **who controls them**

The TV networks are owned by some of the **largest corporations in the world** — NBC is owned by GE, CBS by Viacom, ABC by Disney, Fox by Rupert Murdoch's News Corporation, and CNN by Time Warner. The members of the boards of directors of these corporations also sit on the boards of **weapons manufacturers** and other companies with **vested interests** around the world, such as Boeing, Coca-Cola, Texaco, Chevron, EDS, Lucent, Daimler-Chrysler, Citigroup, Xerox, Philip Morris, Worldcom, JP Morgan Chase, Rockwell Automation, and Honeywell.

Our networks tell you everything you **need to know**

(147)

XEROX   **Honeywell**   *CHRYSLER*   *BOEING*   **Rockwell Automation**

In fact, the corporations that control the television industry are fully integrated into the **military-industrial complex.**

For example, let's take a look at the **media empire** of one of America's premier military contractors— **General Electric**

GE has **major investments** around the world, which it expects the Pentagon to protect. It is also a **charter member** of the military-industrial complex.

A member in good standing, I might add!

GE is the country's third largest military contractor, **raking in billions** of dollars every year. It produces parts for every nuclear weapon in the U.S. arsenal, makes jet engines for military aircraft, and creates all kinds of **profitable electronic gadgets** for the Pentagon. It's also the company that secretly released **millions of curies** of deadly radiation from the Hanford nuclear weapons facility in Washington state and produced **faulty nuclear power plants** that dot the U.S. countryside.

"We bring good things to life!"

Top executives at GE have long been aware that in order to keep billions of Pentagon dollars flowing into its coffers it was necessary to **build public support** for massive military spending. In 1950, President Truman named Charles Wilson, GE's board chairman, to head the **Office of Defense Mobilization**. In that capacity, Wilson told members of the **Newspaper Publishers Association**:

(148)

"If the people were not convinced [that the Free World is in **mortal danger**] it would be impossible for Congress to vote the **vast sums** now being spent to avert this danger. With the support of public opinion, as **marshalled by the press**, we are off to a good start. It is our job — yours and mine — to **keep our people convinced** that the only way to keep disaster away from our shores is to **build up America's might**."

Charles Wilson, 1950

(Of course, Wilson and his buddies at GE expected to get their hands on a **hefty chunk** of those vast sums.)

Under Wilson, GE got into the media business itself to promote its **pro-war message**. In 1954, it hired a **floundering actor** named Ronald Reagan to be its **corporate spokesman**. GE furnished Reagan with an all-electric house and gave him his own TV show, which was called **"GE Theater."**

It also furnished Reagan with **"The Speech,"** GE's political message for America, and sent him around the country to deliver it. He continued to deliver variations of "The Speech" throughout his career.

(149)

Meanwhile, GE was busy **buying up** TV and radio stations across the country.

Then in 1986, GE bought **its own TV network — NBC.**

(150)

> Good evening, I'm **Tom Brokaw** and this is the NBC Nightly News.

General Electric and the other huge corporations that own the news media are **hardly unbiased sources** of information. Yet most of the news available to us — about war and peace and everything else — is **filtered through their perspective**. This gives them a powerful influence on public opinion.

> **Everyone** is rallying behind the President

> Hmmm...

> But their influence is not as complete as they **might hope.**

Chapter 8
Resisting Militarism

In fact, there's been **strong opposition** to foreign military adventures since the Mexican-American and Spanish-American wars of the 19th century. The **anti-war movement** grew especially strong during the war to conquer the Philippines.

" I have seen that we do not intend to free but to **subjugate** the Philippines. And so I am an **anti-imperialist**. I am opposed to having the **eagle put its talons on any other land**... I have a strong aversion to sending our bright boys out there to fight with a **disgraced musket** under a **polluted flag.**"

Mark Twain,
Vice President,
Anti-Imperialist League,
1900

Let's go back to Charles Wilson's era, when he and the media were **mobilizing support** for the **Korean War.** At first they were very successful. But despite their impressive efforts, the support **didn't last long.** After the body bags started coming home, the majority of people turned against the war.

I want my son back home! Now.

The government and the media once again did their best to whip up support for the war in Vietnam. But as the **war escalated,** the greatest anti-war movement in U.S. history arose. At first, the opposition was **small but determined.**

BRING OUR MEN HOME

But opposition **grew by leaps and bounds** as people began to learn what was going on in Vietnam. By 1969 there were 750,000 people **marching on Washington,** and millions more marching in cities across the country.

In May 1970, after police and National Guard troops **fired on anti-war demonstrations,** killing four students at Kent State in Ohio and two students at Jackson State in Mississippi, students at 400 universities across the country went on strike – the **first general student strike** in U.S. history. (152)

When police shot and killed three people during the **Chicano Moratorium** against the war in August 1971, a rebellion raged through East Los Angeles for three days. (153)

Resistance to the war took many forms. People **refused to pay war taxes.**

Paycheck

People burned their draft cards.

Hell no, we won't go!

SELECTIVE SERVICE

The most famous **draft resister** was Muhammad Ali.

I won't serve in a **white man's war!**

People **blocked the path of trains** hauling troops and munitions bound for the war.

STOP THE WAR!
STOP THE TRAIN

14,000 people were arrested when they moved to **shut down Washington, D.C.,** for three days in 1971.

It was the largest mass arrest in U.S. history!

(154)

Even more serious for the Pentagon, **discipline was breaking down** among the troops in Vietnam. The soldiers saw no reason to fight, and they wouldn't. By the end of the '60s, a **virtual civil war** simmered between soldiers and officers. A U.S. military expert warned the Pentagon about the state of its army:

(155) (156)

"[By] every conceivable indicator, our army that now remains in Vietnam is in a state **approaching collapse,** with individual units avoiding or having **refused combat, murdering their officers** and non-commissioned officers, drug-ridden and dispirited where not **near mutinous.**"

Col. Robert Heinl,
U.S.M.C. retired, 1971

FTA

Record numbers of soldiers and sailors **deserted or went AWOL.** Organized resistance was developing among the troops. Hundreds of **underground G.I. newspapers** were springing up at bases around the U.S. and around the world. Contingents of soldiers and sailors were marching at the head of anti-war demonstrations.

Soldiers coming home from Vietnam were telling the country about the **horrors of the war** and they were organizing to stop it. In April 1971, more than a thousand **Vietnam veterans** gathered at the Capitol Building in Washington and **threw back the medals** they had received in the war.

(157)

By the end of the decade, the majority of the people were **against the war.**

The **anti-war movement**, together with the **struggles** waged by African Americans, Latinos, Native Americans, and other oppressed peoples in the U.S., and the women's liberation movement were opening people's eyes to **a whole system of injustice.**

The NLF VIET C... NEVER CALLED us NIGGER

The growing opposition to the war played an important role in convincing the government that it **had to pull out** of Vietnam.

"The **weakest chink in our armor** is American public opinion. Our people won't stand firm in the face of heavy losses, and they can **bring down the government.**"

President Lyndon Johnson, 1968

(158)

As a result of the Vietnam War, a broad anti-militarist sentiment developed among the American people, which was derisively called the **"Vietnam Syndrome"** in official circles.

Don't talk about that **dreadful** disease!

Because U.S. leaders knew that Americans would not stand for large numbers of U.S. war casualties, they had to **restrain their military impulse.** They kept on bombing other countries, but for almost two decades they did not send large numbers of U.S. soldiers to fight on foreign soil.

Until 1991...

Then when George H.W. Bush did send hundreds of thousands of U.S. troops to the Persian Gulf, people were **very apprehensive.** The majority did not want to go to war. A powerful anti-war movement grew more quickly than ever before in U.S. history.

Soon the **streets were filled** with demonstrations.

Immediately after the war began, hundreds of thousands of people marched in San Francisco and Washington, D.C.

George the Elder knew he had to finish the war quickly and with few U.S. casualties or the people would **turn against it.** When Iraq chose to withdraw rather than fight and the war ended with a **one-sided slaughter,** Bush was **euphoric.**

"**By God,** we've kicked the **Vietnam Syndrome** once and for all!"

AMERICA IS NO. 1 - AND DON'T YOU FORGET IT!

(159)

After 9-11, George W. Bush set out to test his father's proposition. He promised us a **long and bloody** "War on Terrorism."

(160)

"So long as anybody's terrorizing established governments, there **needs to be a war**"

George W. Bush October 17, 2001

Americans were stunned by the **horror** of the September 11 attacks and Bush's bellicose words resonated among many. But others were **not so easily led.**

Thousands march to protest U.S. war plans for Afghanistan, Washington, D.C., Sept. 2001

Then as Bush was gearing up to invade Iraq, hundreds of thousands of people **took to the streets** across the country. It soon became clear that the **Vietnam Syndrome** was alive and well— a huge part of the population remained profoundly skeptical about **foreign military adventures**.

Many of the country's largest **labor unions** and **church federations** resolved to oppose the war. Over **150 cities**, including New York, Los Angeles, Chicago, Philadelphia, Detroit, San Francisco and Cleveland went on record opposing the war.

"Empty Warheads Found in Washington"
The Real Smokin' Gun.

NO WAR IN IRAQ

That **never** happened before—not even in the 1960s!

Regime change begins at home!

The whole world was angry. On **February 15 and 16, 2003,** millions of people in the U.S. and over sixty other countries participated in the **largest international protest in history.**

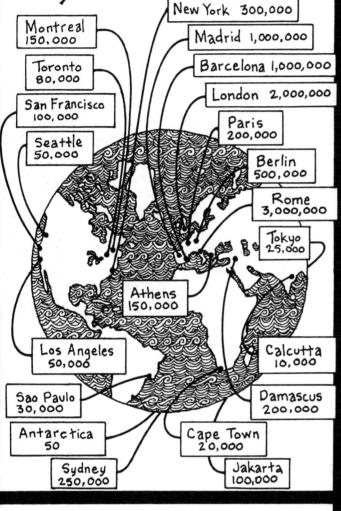

New York 300,000
Montreal 150,000
Madrid 1,000,000
Toronto 80,000
Barcelona 1,000,000
San Francisco 100,000
London 2,000,000
Seattle 50,000
Paris 200,000
Berlin 500,000
Rome 3,000,000
Tokyo 25,000
Athens 150,000
Los Angeles 50,000
Calcutta 10,000
Sao Paulo 30,000
Damascus 200,000
Antarctica 50
Cape Town 20,000
Sydney 250,000
Jakarta 100,000

The great majority of Americans were **not at all eager** to go to war. Most people told pollsters they opposed invading Iraq if Bush could not win U.N. support or if a war would result in large numbers of casualties among U.S. troops or Iraqi civilians. After Bush launched the invasion, however, the **pro-war media blitz** convinced many people that they shouldn't oppose the war because that might endanger U.S. soldiers. (161)

The media forgot to mention that it was Bush who **put us in danger** in the first place.

And that the best way to get us out of danger is to **get us out of here!**

There were a few pro-war rallies, but not many people showed up.

Turn Baghdad into a **parking lot!**

Operation
Iraqi
Liberation

The war ended up **polarizing** the American population and **isolating** the United States internationally. And the **ugly reality** of the American occupation of Iraq has further alienated people here and around the world.

Don't they know that **God** is on **our** side?

The Next Chapter
Do Something About It!

Here are **a few groups** that are trying to figure that out...

We've only been able to include in this list a small number of the many groups conducting anti-militarist education and organizing anti-war activities in the U.S. The movement is growing rapidly and is very diverse. Some of the most vibrant organizations are fledgling, local groups that we were not able to include here. More organizations are listed on Frank Dorrel's website (www.addictedto-war.com). We encourage you to contact groups whose activities are most closely aligned with your own concerns, beliefs, and talents.

American Friends Service Committee

1501 Cherry Street, Philadelphia, PA 19102
Tel: 215-241-7000; Fax: 215-241-7177
Email: afscinfo@afsc.org
Website: www.afsc.org

Formed in 1917, AFSC is a Quaker organization that includes people of various faiths committed to humanitarian service. We believe in the worth of every person and have faith in the power of love to overcome violence and injustice. Programs in the U.S., Africa, Asia, Europe, Latin America, and the Middle East focus on issues related to economic and social justice, youth, peace-building and demilitarization.

Democracy Now! with Amy Goodman

87 Lafayette, New York, NY 10013
Tel: 212-431-9272
Email: mail@democracynow.org
Website: www.democracynow.org

Democracy Now! is a national radio and TV show committed to bringing the voices of the marginalized to the airwaves to discuss global and local issues, including militarism. *Democracy Now!* is broadcast on the Pacifica radio network (KPFA, 94.1 FM, Berkeley; KPFK, 90.7 FM, Los Angeles; KPFT, 90.1 FM, Houston; WBAI, 99.5 FM, New York; WPFW, 89.3 FM, Washington, DC) and on other community radio stations, Free Speech TV (Dish Network Channel 9415), and public access television stations.

G.I. Rights Hotline

Tel: 800-394-9544; 215-563-4620 (overseas calls)
Email: girights@objector.org
Website: www.girights.org

G.I. Rights Hotline provides information to members of the military about discharges, grievance and complaint procedures, and other civil rights. It helps those who are AWOL/UA, victims of harassment and discrimination, and anyone who wants to get out of the military.

Central Committee of Conscientious Objectors

1515 Cherry Street, Philadelphia, PA 19102
Tel: 215-563-8787; Toll Free: 1-800-NOJROTC
Website: www.objector.org

CCCO promotes individual and collective resistance to war and preparations for war. Since 1948, we have been helping people seek discharge from active military service on grounds of conscientious objection, and providing assistance to those faced with a military draft, enlistment obligations, and registration.

Global Peace Campaign

1047 Naka, Kamogawa, Chiba, Japan 296-0111
Tel: 81-470-97-1011; Fax: 81-470-97-1215
Email: yumik@fine.ocn.ne.jp
Website: www.peace2001.org

Founded after the September 11 attacks, GPC supports anti-war education in the U.S. and Japan. Among its projects have been anti-war billboards and peace ads in major newspapers.

Fellowship of Reconciliation

P.O. Box 271, Nyack, NY 10960
Tel: 845-358-4601; Fax: 845-358-4924
Email: info@forusa.org; Website: www.forusa.org

FOR seeks to replace violence, war, racism, and economic injustice with non-violence, peace, and justice. We are an interfaith organization committed to active non-violence as a transforming way of life and a means of radical change. We educate, train, build coalitions, and engage in non-violent, compassionate actions.

Center on Conscience & War

1830 Connecticut Avenue, NW
Washington, DC 20009
Tel: 202-483-2220; Fax: 202-483-1246
Email: nisbco@nisbco.org
Website: www.nisbco.org

Formed in 1940 by religious organizations, CCW defends the rights of conscientious objectors, opposes conscription, and helps those in the military seeking discharge and those facing a crisis of conscience because of draft registration. Services are provided at no charge to all—U.S. citizens, documented and undocumented immigrants, and citizens in other countries.

Global Exchange

2017 Mission Street #303
San Francisco, CA 94110
Tel: 415-255-7296; Fax: 415-255-7498
Website: www.globalexchange.org

Global Exchange is a not-for-profit international human rights organization. Through diverse programs including reality tours to dozens of countries, fair trade stores, corporate accountability campaigns, anti-war work, and green economy promotion, we seek a paradigm shift from money values and violence to life values and nonviolence.

Peace Action

1819 H. Street NW, Suite #420 and #425,
Washington, DC 20006
Tel: 202-862-9740; Fax: 202-862-9762
Website: www.peace-action.org

PA (formerly SANE/Freeze) works to abolish nuclear weapons, develop a peace-oriented economy, and end the international weapons trade. We promote non-military solutions to international conflicts.

International Action Center

39 W. 14th St. # 206, New York, NY 10011
Tel: 212-633-6646; Fax: 212-633-2889
Email: iacenter@iacenter.org
Website: www.iacenter.org

Founded by former U.S. Attorney General Ramsey Clark, the IAC provides information and organizes resistance to U.S. militarism, war, and corporate greed, linking these issues with struggles against domestic racism and oppression.

Military Families Speak Out

PO Box 549, Jamaica Plain, MA 02130.
Tel: 617-522-9323; Email: mfso@mfso.org
Website: www.mfso.org
Also see: www.bringthemhomenow.org

MFSO is made up of people opposed to war in Iraq who have relatives or loved ones in the military. Starting with 2 families in Nov. 2002, we grew to include over 1,000 families within a year. Together with several veterans groups, we founded the "Bring Them Home NOW! Campaign."

War Resisters League

339 Lafayette Street
New York, NY 10012
Tel: 212-228-0450; Email: wrl@warresisters.org
Website: www.warresisters.org

WRL is a pacifist organization founded in 1923. We believe in using nonviolence to remove all the causes of war. We produce educational resources (including *The Nonviolent Activist* magazine), work in coalition with other peace groups, and provide training in civil disobedience, war tax resistance, and other acts of putting conscience into action.

School of the Americas Watch

PO Box 4566, Washington DC 20017
Tel: 202-234-3440; Fax: 202-636-4505
Website: www.soaw.org

SOAW works in solidarity with the people of Latin America to change oppressive U.S. foreign policies. In particular, we work to close the School of the Americas/Western Hemisphere Institute for Security Cooperation, where the Pentagon trains Latin American military officers in methods of repression and torture.

Office of the Americas

8124 W. 3rd Street, Suite 202
Los Angeles, CA 90048-4309
Tel: 323-852-9808; Email: ooa@igc.org
Website: www.officeoftheamericas.org

OOA is a non-profit corporation dedicated to furthering the cause of justice and peace through broad-*based education* including delegations, participation in television, radio, and print media, and presentations to university and high school classes and civic and religious organizations.

Teaching for Change

PO Box 73038; Washington, DC 20056
Toll Free: 1-800-763-9131
Tel: 202-588-7204; Fax: 202-238-0109
Email: tfe@teachingforchange.org
Website: www.teachingforchange.org

TFC promotes social and economic justice through public education. We provide services and resources in the DC Metro area and nationally for K–12 teachers, parents, and teacher educators, through our catalog, training, and other support.

United for Peace & Justice

PO Box 607
Times Square Station
New York, NY 10108
Tel: 212-868-5545; Fax: 646-723-0996
Website: www.unitedforpeace.org

We, the members of UFPJ, stand opposed to the "pre-emptive" wars of aggression waged by the Bush administration; we reject its drive to expand U.S. control over other nations and strip us of our rights at home under the cover of fighting terrorism and spreading democracy; we say NO to its use of war and racism to concentrate power in the hands of the few, at home and abroad.

Not in Our Name

Tel: 212-969-8058
Email: info@notinourname.net
Website: www.notinourname.net

NION is a creative coalition of anti-war activists that has grown into one of the most formidable resistance efforts since the Vietnam War. The NION Pledge of Resistance was created to inspire protest and show solidarity with the people of nations harmed by U.S. militarism.

Coalition Against Militarism In Our Schools

Tel: 626-799-9118
Email: info@militaryfreeschools.org
Website: www.militaryfreeschools.org

CAMS is a grassroots coalition of students, parents, teachers and over 50 organizations based in the Los Angeles area dedicated to demilitarize schools and present alternatives for youth that values life, social justice and peace. CAMS is a member of the National Network Opposed to the Militarization of Youth (NNOMY).

True Majority

PO Box 1976, Old Chelsea Station
New York, NY 10113-1976
Tel: 212-243-3416
Website: www.truemajority.com

TM, led by Ben Cohen (founder of Ben and Jerry's), monitors Congress on social and environmental issues. When your voice needs to be heard, you get an e-mail alert; by clicking reply you send a fax to your congressperson. We seek to ease the nuclear nightmare, renounce the militarization of space, and make globalization work for, not against, working people.

Veterans for Peace

216 S. Meramec Ave.
St. Louis, MO. 63130
Tel: 314-725-6005; Email: vfp@igc.org
Website: www.veteransforpeace.org

VFP is an organization of men and women who served in the military and are now working to abolish war. We educate our fellow citizens about the true costs of militarism, work to change our nation's priorities, and conduct projects to heal the wounds of war.

Women's International League for Peace and Freedom

1213 Race Street, Philadelphia, PA 19107
Tel: 215-563-7110; Fax: 215-563-5527
Email: wilpf@wilpf.org
Website: www.wilpf.org

WILPF works through peaceful means to achieve world disarmament, full rights for women, racial and economic justice, and an end to all forms of violence. We seek to establish political, social, and psychological conditions that can assure peace, freedom, and justice for all.

Reference Notes

1. For updated information on the U.S. military budget, see the Center for Defense Information website (www.cdi.org). Discretionary spending is money that must be specifically appropriated by Congress every year, as opposed to mandatory budget items, such as social security benefits and interest payments on the national debt.

2. Giles cited in Howard Zinn, *A People's History of the United States* (New York: Harper-Collins, 1980), p. 153.

3. Zinn, pp. 125–146; Dee Brown, *Bury My Heart at Wounded Knee: An Indian History of the American West* (New York: Holt, Rinehart and Winston, 1971).

4. Black Elk cited in Brown, p. 419.

5. Zinn, pp. 147–166.

6. Denby cited in David Healy, *U.S. Expansionism: The Imperialist Urge in the 1890s* (Madison, WI: University of Wisconsin Press, 1970), pp. 122–123.

7. Platt cited in Healy, p. 173.

8. Roosevelt cited in Zinn, p. 290.

9. Zinn, pp. 290–305; Beveridge cited in Zinn, p. 306.

10. Beveridge cited in Healy, p. 174.

11. Beveridge cited in Rubin Westin, *Racism in U.S. Imperialism* (Columbia, SC: University of South Carolina Press, 1972), p. 46.

12. Zinn, pp. 305–313; Michael Parenti, *The Sword and the Dollar* (New York: St. Martins Press, 1989), pp. 42–43.

13. Zinn, pp. 290–305.

14. Hawaii: Joseph Gerson, "The Sun Never Sets," in Joseph Gerson, ed., *The Sun Never Sets—Confronting the Network of Foreign U.S. Military Bases* (Boston: South End Press, 1991), pp. 6, 10; Panama: T. Harry Williams, et al., *A History of the United States [Since 1865]*, 2nd edition (New York: Alfred Knopf, 1965), pp. 372–373.

15. David Cooney, *A Chronology of the U.S. Navy: 1775–1965* (New York: Franklin Watts, 1965), pp. 181–257.

16. Catherine Sunshine, *The Caribbean: Struggle, Survival and Sovereignty* (Boston: South End Press, 1985), p. 32.

17. George Black, *The Good Neighbor* (New York: Pantheon Books, 1988), pp. 31–58; Sunshine, pp. 28–34.

18. Taft cited in William Appleman Williams, *Americans in a Changing World* (New York: Harper and Row, 1978), pp. 123–124.

19. Newspaper report cited in Westin, p. 226.

20. Sunshine, p. 83.

21. This and subsequent passages are from Smedley Butler, *War Is a Racket* (New York: Round Table Press, 1935); reproduced at: www.veteransforpeace.org/ war_is_a_racket_033103.htm.

22. Page cited in William Foster, *Outline Political History of the Americas* (New York: International Publishers, 1951), p. 362.

23. Foster, p. 360.

24. CFR/State Department policy statement cited in Lawrence Shoup and William Minter, *Imperial Brain Trust: The Council on Foreign Relations and U.S. Foreign Policy* (New York: Monthly Review, 1977), p. 130.

25. CFR memorandum cited in Shoup and Minter, p. 170.

26. *Hiroshima-Nagasaki: A Pictorial Record of the Atomic Destruction* (Tokyo: Hiroshima-Nagasaki Publishing Committee, 1978), p. 17.

27. Truman cited in Paul Boyer, *By the Bombs Early Light: American Thought and Culture at the Dawn of the Atomic Age* (New York: Pantheon, 1985).

28. The bombing was also intended to preempt Soviet involvement in the war against Japan: Zinn, pp. 413–415.

29. Welch cited in Victor Perlo, *Militarism and Industry: Arms Profiteering in the Missile Age* (New York: International Publishers, 1963), p. 144.

30. Gerson, p. 12.

31. Korea International War Crimes Tribunal, *Report on U.S. Crimes in Korea: 1945–2001*, (Washington, D.C.: Korea Truth Commission Task Force, 2001), p. xi; *Encyclopedia Britannica*, 1967 ed., v. 13, p. 475; U.S. Dept. of Defense, *Selected Manpower Statistics, Fiscal Year 1984* (Washington D.C., 1985), p. 111.

32. Sunshine, p. 142; Black, p. 118.

33. Noam Chomsky, "Patterns of Intervention," in Joseph Gerson, ed., *The Deadly Connection: Nuclear War and U.S. Intervention* (Philadelphia: New Society, 1986), p. 66; Zinn, p. 469; Sean Murphy et al., *No Fire, No Thunder: The Threat of Chemical and Biological Weapons* (New York: Monthly Review, 1984), pp. 22–24, 64, 78–79; Parenti, p. 44; U.S. Dept. of Defense, *Selected Manpower Statistics*; Marilyn Young, *The Vietnam Wars: 1945–1990* (New York: Harper-Collins, 1991).

34. Robert Fisk, *Pity the Nation: Lebanon at War* (Oxford: Oxford University Press, 1992); Sandra Mackey, *Lebanon: Death of a Nation* (New York: Congdon & Weed, 1989).

35. Black, p. 156.

36. Schultz cited in Black, p. 156.

37. Noam Chomsky, *The Culture of Terrorism* (Boston: South End Press, 1988), p. 29; Associated Press, "Libyan Court Wants Americans Arrested for 1986 Bombing," March 22, 1999.

38. Noam Chomsky, *Fateful Triangle: The United States, Israel & The Palestinians* (Cambridge, MA: South End Press, 1999).

39. William Blum, *Killing Hope: U.S. Military and CIA Interventions Since World War II* (Monroe, ME: Common Courage Press, 1995).

40. Jack Nelson-Pallmeyer, *School of Assassins* (Maryknoll, NY: Orbis Books, 1999).

41. Charles Bergquist, et al., *Violence in Colombia: The Contemporary Crisis in Historical Perspective* (Wilmington, DE: Scholarly Resources, 1992); W. M. Leo Grande and K. Sharpe, "A Plan, But No Clear Objective," *Washington Post*, April 1, 2001; Mark Cook, "Colombia, the Politics of Escalation," *Covert Action Quarterly*, Fall/Winter 1999.

42. Peter Wyden, *Bay of Pigs: The Untold Story* (New York: Simon and Schuster, 1979).

43. Richard Leonard, *South Africa at War: White Power and the Crisis in Southern Africa* (Westport, CT: Lawrence Hill, 1983); Richard Bloomfield, ed., *Regional Conflict and U.S. Policy: Angola and Mozambique* (Algonac, MI: Reference Publications, 1988); Alex Vines, *RENAMO: Terrorism and Mozambique* (Bloomington, IN: Indiana University Press, 1991); Joseph Hanlon and James Currey, *Mozambique: Who Calls the Shots?* (London: Zed, 1991).

44. Reagan cited in Black, p. 170.

45. John K. Cooley, *Unholy Wars: Afghanistan, America and International Terrorism* (London: Pluto Press, 2000).

46. Chalmers Johnson, "American Militarism and Blowback," in Carl Boggs, ed., *Masters of War: Militarism and Blowback in the Era of American Empire* (New York: Routledge, 2003), pp. 113–115.

47. National Security Council document cited in *New York Times*, Feb. 23, 1991.

48. Doug Ireland, "Press Clips," *Village Voice*, Nov. 13, 1990.

49. Tim Wheeler, "Reagan, Noriega and Citicorp," *People's Daily World*, Feb. 25, 1988.

50. Kenneth Sharpe and Joseph Treaster, "Cocaine Is Again Surging Out of Panama," *New York Times*, Aug. 13, 1991.

51. Tom Wicker, "What Price Panama?," *New York Times*, June 15, 1990; Nathaniel Sheppard, Jr., "Year Later, Panama Still Aches," *Chicago Tribune*, Dec. 16, 1990, p. 1; Associated Press, "Ex-Senator Says U.S. Massacred Panamanians" *Chicago Tribune*, Nov. 15, 1990.

52. Daniel Yergin, *The Prize: The Epic Quest for Oil, Money, and Power* (New York: Simon and Schuster, 1991), pp. 200–202; Michel Moushabeck, "Iraq: Years of Turbulence," in Phyllis Bennis and Michel Moushabeck, eds., *Beyond the Storm: A Gulf Crisis Reader* (New York: Olive Branch Press, 1991), pp. 26–28.

53. State Department statement cited in Joseph Gersen, et al., "The U.S. in the Middle East," in Gersen, ed., *Deadly Connection*, p. 167.

54. Michael Tanzer, *The Energy Crisis: World Struggle for Power and Wealth* (New York: Monthly Review, 1974).

55. The Ba'ath Party was soon thrown out of the government, but came back to power in a 1968 coup that was also aided by the CIA (Roger Morris, "A Tyrant 40 Years in the Making," *New York Times*, March 14, 2003; Moushabeck, pp. 29–30).

56. Kissinger cited in Hans von Sponek and Denis Halliday, "The Hostage Nation," *The Guardian*, Nov. 29, 2001.

57. Alan Friedman, *Spider's Web: The Secret History of How the White House Illegally Armed Iraq* (New York: Bantam Books, 1993); Clyde Farnsworth, "Military Exports to Iraq Under Scrutiny, Congressional Aides Say," *New York Times*, June 24, 1991; Michael Klare, "Behind Desert Storm: The New Military Paradigm," *Technology Review*, May–June 1991, p. 36; Philip Shenon, "Iraq Links Germs for Weapons to U.S. and France," *New York Times*, March 16, 2003.

58. Christopher Dickey and Evan Thomas, "How Saddam Happened," *Newsweek*, Sept. 23, 2002; Elaine Sciolino, "Iraq Chemical Arms Condemned, But West Once Looked the Other Way," *New York Times*, February 13, 2003.

59. Philip Green "Who Really Shot Down Flight 655?" *The Nation*, Aug. 13–20, 1988, pp. 125–126.

60. Bush cited in Yergin, p. 773.

61. Hitchins; Bush cited in *Newsweek*, Jan. 7, 1991, p.19.

62. Michael Klare, "High Death Weapons of the Gulf War," *The Nation*, June 3, 1991; Malcolm Browne, "Allies Are Said to Choose Napalm for Strikes on Iraqi Fortifications," *New York Times*, Feb. 23, 1991; John Donnelly, "Iraqi cancers offer clues to Gulf War Syndrome: Uranium residue a prime suspect," *Miami Herald*, April 6, 1998.

63. Bush cited in Mitchel Cohen, "'What We Say Goes!': How Bush Senior Sold the Bombing of Iraq," *Counterpunch*, Dec. 28, 2002.

64. Middle East Watch, *Needless Deaths in the Gulf War: Civilian Casualties During the Air Campaign and Violations of the Laws of War* (New York: Human Rights Watch, 1991); Mark Fireman, "Eyewitnesses Report Misery, Devastation in the Cities of Iraq," *Seattle Times*, Feb. 5, 1991; George Esper, "500 Die in Bombed Shelter in Baghdad," *Chicago Sun Times*, Feb. 13, 1991; David Evans, "Study: Hyperwar Devastated Iraq," *Chicago Tribune*, May 29, 1991.

65. "War Summary: Closing the Gate," *New York Times*, Feb. 28, 1991; Associated Press, "Army Tanks Buried Iraqi Soldiers Alive," *Greeley Tribune*, Sept. 12, 1991.

66. Bush cited in Robert Borosage, "How Bush kept the guns from turning into butter," *Rolling Stone*, Feb. 21, 1991, p. 20.

67. Ramsey Clark, *The Fire This Time: U.S. War Crimes in the Gulf* (New York: International Action Center, 2002), pp. 64–64, 209; Thomas Nagy, "The Secret Behind the Sanctions: How the U.S. Intentionally Destroyed Iraq's Water Supply," *The Progressive*, Sept. 2001.

68. John Pilger, "Collateral Damage," in Anthony Arnove, ed., *Iraq Under Siege: The Deadly Impact of Sanctions and War* (Cambridge, MA: South End Press, 2000), pp. 59–66.

69. Noam Chomsky, *A New Generation Draws the Line: Kosovo, East Timor and the Standards of the West* (London: Verso, 2001), p. 11.

70. Nick Wood, "U.S. 'Covered Up' for Kosovo Ally," *London Observer*, Sept. 10, 2000; Norman Kempster, "Crisis in Yugoslavia, Rebel Force May Prove to be a Difficult Ally," *Los Angeles Times*, April 1, 1999; Diana Johnstone, "Hawks and Eagles: 'Greater NATO' Flies to the Aid of 'Greater Albania,'" *Covert Action Quarterly*, Spring/Summer, 1999, p. 6–12.

71. Noam Chomsky, *The New Military Humanism: Lessons from Kosovo* (Monroe, ME: Common Courage Press, 1999).

72. Bin Laden cited in *Wall Street Journal*, Oct. 7, 2001.

73. Bush cited in "The President's Words," *The Los Angeles Times*, Sept. 22, 2001.

74. Bosch cited in Alexander Cockburn, "The Tribulations of Joe Doherty," *Wall Street Journal*, reprinted in the *Congressional Record*, Aug. 3, 1990, p. E2639.

75. Ibid; John Rice, "Man with CIA Links Accused of Plotting to Kill Castro," Associated Press, Nov. 18, 2000; Frances Robles and Glenn Garvin, "Four Held in Plot Against Castro," *Miami Herald*, Nov. 19, 2000; Jill Mullin, "The Burden of a Violent History," *Miami New Times*, April 20, 2000.

76. Joe Conason, "The Bush Pardons," http://archive. salon.com/news/col/cona/2001/02/27/pardons/.

77. Bosch cited in Cockburn.

78. Blum.

79. A limited field investigation documented 824 civilian deaths caused by the U.S.-led bombing campaign (www.globalexchange.org/countries/afghanistan/apogr eport.pdf). A more comprehensive investigation based on press reports estimated that U.S. bombs killed between 3100 and 3600 Afghan civilians (Marc Herold, "U.S. bombing and Afghan civilian deaths: The official neglect of unworthy bodies," *International Journal of Urban and Regional Research*, Sept. 2002, pp. 626–634; also see: http://pubpages.unh.edu/~mwherold). Many more died because the bombing cut off relief supplies.

80. Seymour Hersh, "The Other War: Why Bush's Afghanistan problem won't go away," *New Yorker,* April 12, 2004.

81. Bush cited in Barry Horstman, "We cannot wait for a mushroom cloud," *Cincinnati Post*, Oct. 8, 2002.

82. For a review of the manipulation of evidence, see Sheldon Rampton and John Stauber, *Weapons of Mass Deception: The Uses of Propaganda in Bush's War on Iraq* (JP Tarcher, July 2003). The broader purposes of the U.S. invasion of Iraq were advanced in a policy paper, *Rebuilding America's Defenses*, published by the Project for a New American Century in September 2000. PNAC members Dick Cheney, Donald Rumsfeld, Paul Wolfowitz, and Richard Perle, became key members of the incoming Bush Administration and the paper became a blueprint for the administration's aggressive foreign policy. The authors declared: "The United States has for decades sought to play a more permanent role in Gulf regional security. While the unresolved conflict with Iraq provides the immediate justification, the need for a substantial American force presence in the Gulf transcends the issue of the regime of Saddam Hussein." The paper can be found at: www.newamericancentury.org.

83. An Associated Press research team surveyed the records of 60 Iraqi hospitals (less than half the total number) and found unambiguous evidence of at least 3,240 war-related civilian deaths (Niko Price, "First Tally Puts Iraqi Civilian Deaths at 3240," *Atlanta Journal-Constitution*, June 10, 2003). A careful survey of press reports indicated that between 9,137 and 10,994 Iraqi civilians had been killed as of mid-May 2004 (www.iraqbodycount.net).

84. Unnamed senior Bush Administration official cited in "Pentagon Expects Long-Term Access to Key Iraq Bases," *New York Times,* April 20, 2003.

85. Pressure to convert Iraq into a base for U.S. troops presumably increased after it became clear that the U.S. military would have to leave Saudi Arabia (see David Rennie, "America to Withdraw Troops from Saudi Arabia," *Telegraph*, April 30, 2003). For a discussion of the strategic importance of oil reserves in Iraq and the rest of the Middle East, see Michael Klare, *Resource Wars: The New Landscape of Global Conflict* (New York: Henry Holt, 2001).

86. Kareem Fahim, "Recalling Ahmed Chalabi," *Village Voice*, April 9-15, 2003; John Cassidy, "Beneath the sand: Can a shattered country be rebuilt with oil?" *New Yorker*, July 14, 2003. Chalabi cited in "In Iraqi War Scenario, Oil Is a Key Issue," *Washington Post*, Sept. 15, 2002. Although Chalabi continues to favor privatization of the oil industry, U.S. officials abandoned the idea of privatization in the oil sphere, at least for now, so as not to fan anti-American sentiments (Chip Cummins, "State-run oil company is being weighed for Iraq," *Wall Street Journal*, Jan. 7, 2004).

87. Powell cited in *The Economist*, April 5, 2003. For an analysis of the results of other instances of "regime change" initiated by the U.S., see William Blum, *Killing Hope: U.S. Military and CIA Interventions Since World War II* (Monroe, ME: Common Courage Press, 1995).

88. Sabrina Tavernise, "U.S. Tells Iraq Oil Ministers Not to Act Without Its OK," *New York Times*, April 30, 2003; "To the victor go the spoils in Iraq Reconstruction," Reuters, April 15, 2003; "The Oil Spoils," *The Nation*, June 16, 2003.

89. Edward Wong, "Direct Election of Iraq Assembly Pushed by Cleric," *New York Times*, Jan. 12, 2004; Steven Weisman, "Bush Team Revising Planning for Iraqi Self-Rule," *New York Times*, Jan. 13, 2004. Bremer cited in Booth and Chandrasekaran, "Occupation Forces Halting Elections Throughout Iraq" *Washington Post*, June 28, 2003.

90. Seymour Hersh, "Torture at Abu Ghraib," *New Yorker*, May 10, 2004. Prisoners held by the U.S. military in Afghanistan and in Guantánamo, Cuba were treated in similar fashion, indicating systemic practices of torture and abuse approved at the highest levels (Seymour Hersh, "The Gray Zone" *New Yorker*, May 24, 2004.)

91. Ashcroft continued: "[W]e will help make that freedom permanent by assisting them to establish an equitable criminal justice system based on the rule of law and standards of basic human rights." One of the team selected by Ashcroft, Lane McCotter, had been forced to resign as director of Utah prisons after a prisoner abuse scandal. He was assigned to rehabilitate Hussein's infamous Abu Ghraib prison, which soon gained renewed notoriety in American hands (Fox Butterfield, "Mistreatment of Prisoners Is Called Routine in U.S.," *New York Times*, May 8, 2004).

92. Alex Gourevitch, "Exporting Censorship to Iraq," *American Prospect*, Oct. 1, 2003; Amnesty International, *Iraq: One Year On the Human Rights Situation Remains Dire* (web.amnesty.org)

93. Bush cited in "U.S. Attributes Explosion at Iraqi Mosque to Bomb-Making Activity," *New York Times*, July 3, 2003.

94. BBC News, "Picture Emerges of Falluja Siege," April 23, 2004 (www.bbc.co.uk).

95. Unnamed American soldier quoted in David Rhode, "Search for Guns in Iraq and Surprise Under a Robe," *New York Times*, June 3, 2003.

96. Thom Shanker, "Rumsfeld Doubles Estimate For Cost of Troops in Iraq; General Says U.S. Expects to Keep Force at 145,000 'For the Foreseeable Future,'" *New York Times*, July 10, 2003. As of May 14, 2004, U.S. military casualties in Iraq since March 2003 had reached 782 dead and more than 4490 wounded; U.S. military deaths in Afghanistan since October 2001 had reached 119 (for updated numbers, see: www.antiwar.com).

97. Unnamed member of a group of CIA and Special Forces paramilitary operatives cited in Bob Woodward, *Bush at War* (New York: Simon and Schuster, 2002), p. 352.

98. For updated information on U.S. military contracts, see the Center for Defense Information's website: www.cdi.org.

99. Hartung.

100. Robert Bryce, "The Candidate from Brown & Root," *The Austin Chronicle,* Aug. 25, 2000.

101. Jane Mayer, "Contract Sport: What did the Vice-President do for Halliburton?" *New Yorker*, Feb. 16 &23, 2004.

102. In 2000, Cheney left Halliburton to run for vice-president, but he retained $18 million in stock options and receives about $150,000 a year in deferred compensation (Mayer).

103. Katherine Seelye, "Cheney's Five Draft Deferments During the Vietnam Era Emerge as a Campaign Issue," *New York Times*, May 1, 2004; Jon Wiener, "Hard to Muzzle: The Return of Lynne Cheney," *The Nation*, Oct. 2, 2000.

104. Seymour Hersh, "Lunch with the Chairman: Why was Richard Perle Meeting with Adnan Khashoggi?" *New Yorker*, March 17, 2003, pp. 76–81.

105. See, for instance, a 1996 policy proposal entitled, "A Clean Break: A New Strategy for Securing the Realm" penned by a group of neo-conservative strategists led by Perle for the Netanyahu government in Israel. The proposal can be seen at: www.israeleconomy.org/strat1.htm.

106. Robert Higgs, ed., *Arms, Politics and the Economy* (New York: Holmes & Meier, 1980), Preface, p. xiii.

107. The 1972 Anti-Ballistic Missile Treaty had outlawed defensive missile systems. See Joshua Cohen, "An Interview with Ted Postol: What's Wrong with Missile Defense," *Boston Review*, Oct./Nov. 2001; David Sanger, "Washington's New Freedom and New Worries in the Post-ABM-Treaty Era," *New York Times*, Dec. 15, 2001.

108. Paul Richter, "Plan for new nukes clears major hurdle," *Los Angeles Times*, May 10, 2003. For updated information on U.S. nuclear weapons policies see the Physicians for Social Responsibility website: www.psr.org.

109. R. Jeffrey Smith, "U.S. Urged to Cut 50% of A-Arms: Soviet Breakup Is Said to Allow Radical Shift in Strategic Targeting," *Washington Post*, Jan. 6, 1991. Also see Michael Gordon, "U.S. Nuclear Plan Sees New Weapons and New Targets," *New York Times*, March 10, 2002.

110. Judith Miller, "U.S. Seeks Changes in Germ War Pact," *New York Times*, Nov. 1, 2001; William Broad and Judith Miller, "U.S. Recently Produced Anthrax in a Highly Lethal Powder Form," *New York Times*, Dec. 13, 2001.

111. William Broad and Judith Miller, *Germs: Biological Weapons and America's Secret War* (New York: Simon and Schuster, 2001); Blum.

112. Data are from the following years: the U.S., 2004; Japan, 2002; Russia and China, 2001. For updated information on U.S. and world military spending, see the Center for Defense Information website: www.cdi.org.

113. Center for Defense Information, *2001–2002 Military Almanac*, p. 35 (see www.cdi.org). For the 2003 and 2004 fiscal years, Congress approved special appropriations of $166 billion to finance the invasion and occupation of Iraq (David Firestone, "Bush Likely to Get Spending Request, Lawmakers Agree," *New York Times*, Sept. 9, 2003).

114. Center for Defense Information, www.cdi.org/issues/milspend.html.

115. Michael Renner, *National Security: The Economic and Environmental Dimensions* (Washington, D.C.: World Watch Institute, 1989), p. 23.

116. The War Resisters League's annual analysis of total U.S. military expenditures can be found at: www.warresisters.org/piechart.htm.

117. The War Resisters League estimates that about 46% of federal tax revenues are used for military expenses (ibid.). Total 2000 federal individual income tax revenues ($1,004,500,000,000) multiplied by 46%, divided by 104,705,000 households = $4,417. (www.census.gov/prod/2002pubs/01statab/fedgov.pdf, pp. 21 and 305).

118. Timothy Saasta, et al., *America's Third Deficit: Too Little Investment in People and Infrastructure* (Washington, D.C.: Center for Community Change, 1991).

119. Jobs With Peace Campaign, *Fact Sheet No. 3* (Boston, 1990).

120. Saasta; Institute for Policy Studies, *Harvest of Shame: Ten Years of Conservative Misrule* (Washington, D.C.: Institute for Policy Studies, 1991), p. 11; Jane Midgley, *The Women's Budget, 3rd Edition* (Philadelphia: Women's International League for Peace and Freedom, 1989), p. 19.

121. Saasta; Midgley, p. 19.

122. Institute for Policy Studies, p. 11.

123. Midgley, p. 16; Pam Belluck, "New Wave of the Homeless Floods Cities' Shelters," *New York Times*, Dec. 18, 2001.

124. James Dao, "War Mutes Critics of Costly Carrier Groups," *New York Times*, Nov. 11, 2001.

125. Prenatal care costs $625 per mother: U.S. Congress, *Background Material and Data on Programs within the Jurisdiction of the Committee on Ways and Means* (Washington D.C., 1990).

126. The Head Start program costs $2,600 per student annually: U.S. Congress.

127. Private clinics charge about $3,000 per year for intensive outpatient drug or alcohol treatment: Survey by author.

128. Citizens Budget Campaign, *It's Our Budget, It's Our Future* (Washington D.C.).

129. Dao, "War Mutes Critics of Costly Carrier Groups."